Edexcel GCSE (9-1)
History

Anglo-Saxon and Norman England, c1060–1088

Series Editor: Angela Leonard   Author: Rob Bircher

endorsed for
Edexcel

ALWAYS LEARNING   **PEARSON**

Published by Pearson Education Limited, 80 Strand, London, WC2R 0RL.

www.pearsonschoolsandfecolleges.co.uk

Copies of official specifications for all Edexcel qualifications may be found on the website: www.edexcel.com

Text © Pearson Education Limited 2016

Series editor: Angela Leonard
Designed by Colin Tilley Loughrey, Pearson Education Limited
Typeset by Phoenix Photosetting, Chatham, Kent
Original illustrations © Pearson Education Limited
Illustrated by KJA Artists Illustration Agency and Phoenix Photosetting, Chatham, Kent.

Cover design by Colin Tilley Loughrey
Picture research by
Cover photo © Alamy Images: Robert Harding Picture Library Ltd

The right of Rob Bircher to be identified as author of this work has been asserted by him in accordance with the Copyright, Designs and Patents Act 1988.

First published 2016

25 24 23 22 21 20
15 14 13 12 11 10 9 8 7

British Library Cataloguing in Publication Data
A catalogue record for this book is available from the British Library.
ISBN 978 1 292 12723 1

Printed in Slovakia by Neografia

A note from the publisher
In order to ensure that this resource offers high-quality support for the associated Pearson qualification, it has been through a review process by the awarding body. This process confirms that this resource fully covers the teaching and learning content of the specification or part of a specification at which it is aimed. It also confirms that it demonstrates an appropriate balance between the development of subject skills, knowledge and understanding, in addition to preparation for assessment.

Endorsement does not cover any guidance on assessment activities or processes (e.g. practice questions or advice on how to answer assessment questions), included in the resource nor does it prescribe any particular approach to the teaching or delivery of a related course.

While the publishers have made every attempt to ensure that advice on the qualification and its assessment is accurate, the official specification and associated assessment guidance materials are the only authoritative source of information and should always be referred to for definitive guidance.

Pearson examiners have not contributed to any sections in this resource relevant to examination papers for which they have responsibility.

Examiners will not use endorsed resources as a source of material for any assessment set by Pearson.

Endorsement of a resource does not mean that the resource is required to achieve this Pearson qualification, nor does it mean that it is the only suitable material available to support the qualification, and any resource lists produced by the awarding body shall include this and other appropriate resources.

Websites
Pearson Education Limited is not esponsible for the content of any external internet sites. It is essential for tutors to preview each website before using it in class so as to ensure that he URL is still accurate, relevant and appropriate. We suggest that tutors bookmark useful websites and consider enabling students to access them through the school/college intranet.

Contents

How to use this book

What's covered?

This book covers the British Depth study on Anglo-Saxon and Norman England, c1060-88. This unit makes up 20% of your GCSE course, and will be examined in Paper 2.

Depth studies cover a short period of time, and require you to know about society, people and events in detail. You need to understand how the different aspects of the period fit together and affect each other. This book also explains the different types of exam questions you will need to answer, and includes advice and example answers to help you improve.

Features

As well as a clear, detailed explanation of the key knowledge you will need, you will also find a number of features in the book:

Key terms

Where you see a word followed by an asterisk, like this: Ceorls*, you will be able to find a Key Terms box on that page that explains what the word means.

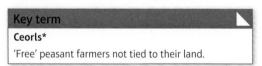

Key term
Ceorls*
'Free' peasant farmers not tied to their land.

Activities

Every few pages, you'll find a box containing some activities designed to help check and embed knowledge and get you to really think about what you've studied. The activities start simple, but might get more challenging as you work through them.

Summaries and Checkpoints

At the end of each chunk of learning, the main points are summarised in a series of bullet points – great for embedding the core knowledge, and handy for revision.

Checkpoints help you to check and reflect on your learning. The Strengthen section helps you to consolidate knowledge and understanding, and check that you've grasped the basic ideas and skills. The Challenge questions push you to go beyond just understanding the information, and into evaluation and analysis of what you've studied.

Sources and Interpretations

Although source work and interpretations do not appear in Paper 2, you'll still find interesting contemporary material throughout the books, showing what people from the period said, thought or created, helping you to build your understanding of people in the past.

The book also includes extracts from the work of historians, showing how experts have interpreted the events you've been studying.

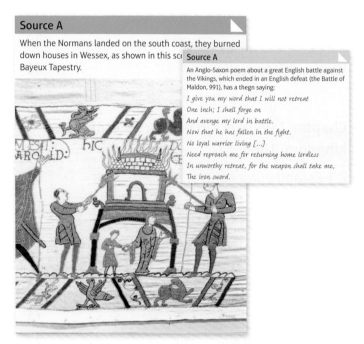

Source A

When the Normans landed on the south coast, they burned down houses in Wessex, as shown in this scene [from the] Bayeux Tapestry.

Source A

An Anglo-Saxon poem about a great English battle against the Vikings, which ended in an English defeat (the Battle of Maldon, 991), has a thegn saying:

I give you my word that I will not retreat
One inch; I shall forge on
And avenge my lord in battle.
Now that he has fallen in the fight.
No loyal warrior living [...]
Need reproach me for returning home lordless
In unworthy retreat, for the weapon shall take me,
The iron sword.

Extend your knowledge

These features contain useful additional information that adds depth to your knowledge, and to your answers. The information is closely related to the key issues in the unit, and questions are sometimes included, helping you to link the new details to the main content.

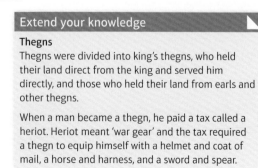

Extend your knowledge

Thegns

Thegns were divided into king's thegns, who held their land direct from the king and served him directly, and those who held their land from earls and other thegns.

When a man became a thegn, he paid a tax called a heriot. Heriot meant 'war gear' and the tax required a thegn to equip himself with a helmet and coat of mail, a horse and harness, and a sword and spear.

Exam-style questions and tips

The book also includes extra exam-style questions you can use to practise. These appear in the chapters and are accompanied by a tip to help you get started on an answer.

Exam-style question, Section B

Describe **two** features of the social system of Anglo-Saxon England.   **4 marks**

Exam tip

This question is about identifying key features. You need to identify two relevant points and then develop each point. For example: 'The social system was not fixed. This meant a free peasant who did very well could become a thegn.'

Recap pages

At the end of each chapter, you'll find a page designed to help you to consolidate and reflect on the chapter as a whole. Each recap page includes a recall quiz, ideal for quickly checking your knowledge or for revision. Recap pages also include activities designed to help you summarise and analyse what you've learned, and also reflect on how each chapter links to other parts of the unit.

THINKING HISTORICALLY

These activities are designed to help you develop a better understanding of how history is constructed, and are focused on the key areas of Evidence, Interpretations, Cause & Consequence and Change & Continuity. In the British Depth Study, you will come across activities on Cause & Consequence, as this is a key focus for this unit.

The Thinking Historically approach has been developed in conjunction with Dr Arthur Chapman and the Institute of Education, UCL. It is based on research into the misconceptions that can hold students back in history.

THINKING HISTORICALLY ▶ Cause and Consequence (3a&b) ——— conceptual map reference

The Thinking Historically conceptual map can be found at: www.pearsonschools.co.uk/thinkinghistoricallygcse

At the end of most chapters is a spread dedicated to helping you improve your writing skills. These include simple techniques you can use in your writing to make your answers clearer, more precise and better focused on the question you're answering.

The Writing Historically approach is based on the *Grammar for Writing* pedagogy developed by a team at the University of Exeter and popular in many English departments. Each spread uses examples from the preceding chapter, so it's relevant to what you've just been studying.

Preparing for your exams

At the back of the book, you'll find a special section dedicated to explaining and exemplifying the new Edexcel GCSE History exams. Advice on the demands of this paper, written by Angela Leonard, helps you prepare for and approach the exam with confidence. Each question type is explained through annotated sample answers at two levels, showing clearly how answers can be improved.

Pearson Progression Scale: This icon indicates the Step that a sample answer has been graded at on the Pearson Progression Scale.

This book is also available as an online ActiveBook, which can be licensed for your whole institution.

There is also an ActiveLearn Digital Service available to support delivery of this book, featuring a front-of-class version of the book, lesson plans, worksheets, exam practise PowerPoints, assessments, notes on Thinking Historically and Writing Historically, and more.

ActiveLearn
Digital Service

Timeline: Anglo-Saxons and Normans

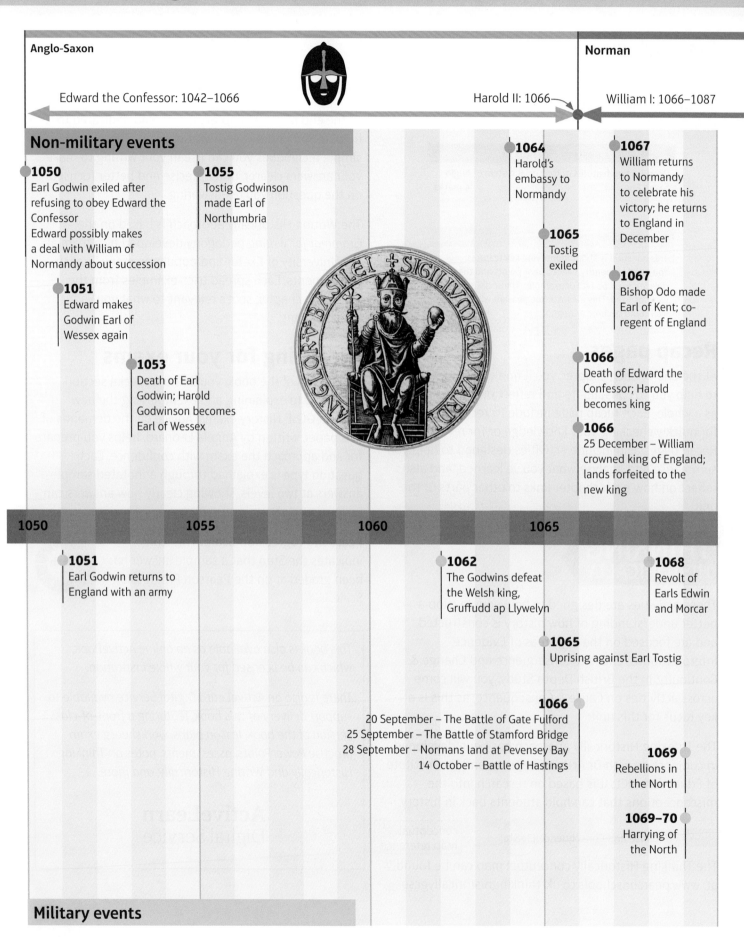

Anglo-Saxon

Norman

Edward the Confessor: 1042–1066

Harold II: 1066

William I: 1066–1087

Non-military events

1050
Earl Godwin exiled after refusing to obey Edward the Confessor
Edward possibly makes a deal with William of Normandy about succession

1051
Edward makes Godwin Earl of Wessex again

1053
Death of Earl Godwin; Harold Godwinson becomes Earl of Wessex

1055
Tostig Godwinson made Earl of Northumbria

1064
Harold's embassy to Normandy

1065
Tostig exiled

1066
Death of Edward the Confessor; Harold becomes king

1066
25 December – William crowned king of England; lands forfeited to the new king

1067
William returns to Normandy to celebrate his victory; he returns to England in December

1067
Bishop Odo made Earl of Kent; co-regent of England

1050   1055   1060   1065

1051
Earl Godwin returns to England with an army

1062
The Godwins defeat the Welsh king, Gruffudd ap Llywelyn

1065
Uprising against Earl Tostig

1066
20 September – The Battle of Gate Fulford
25 September – The Battle of Stamford Bridge
28 September – Normans land at Pevensey Bay
14 October – Battle of Hastings

1068
Revolt of Earls Edwin and Morcar

1069
Rebellions in the North

1069–70
Harrying of the North

Military events

William II (William Rufus): 1087–1100

1070
Stigand replaced by Lanfranc as Archbishop of Canterbury

1071
Edwin's lands forfeited

1076
Inquiry into Bishop Odo's illegal land grabs

1080
Robert and William reconciled

1082
Bishop Odo imprisoned

1083
Death of Matilda, William's wife and trusted regent

1084
Heavy geld tax levied

1085
William orders Domesday Book surveys

1086
First drafts of the Domesday Book shown to William; landholders summoned to swear allegiance

1087
Death of William in Normandy William II (William Rufus) crowned king of England

| 1070 | 1075 | 1080 | 1085 | 1090 |

1070–71
Hereward the Wake and the revolt at Ely

1075
Revolt of the Earls

1077
Robert Curthose rebels against his father, William

1085
Threat of Danish invasion means William brings thousands more troops into England

1088
Odo leads rebellion against William Rufus, which is defeated

01 | Anglo-Saxon England and the Norman Conquest, 1060–66

By the time of King Edward the Confessor (1042–66), England had been mostly under the control of Anglo-Saxons for 600 years. Through those centuries, England had developed a very strong government. It also had a prosperous economy, boosted by extensive trade links across the North Sea and the Channel. England was a Christian country, but Christian teachings were mixed with ancient beliefs about how people should behave. One key belief was that, in return for protection from a lord, his people owed him service. For example, in return for land to farm, a man would owe military service to his lord.

England had faced a terrible threat for centuries: the Vikings. These were Scandinavians who had raided settlements all along the coasts of Europe. In England, their raids were followed by invasions, so that many parts of northern England had Viking settlers. The kings before Edward had been Vikings: Cnut and his two sons. One of the reasons that England had a very well-organised government was because of the need for all Anglo-Saxons to work together to deal with the Vikings. The way Christian belief had developed was also connected to the threat of invasion. People understood Viking raids as punishment from God for the sins of the English people. The Church said that the only way to prevent further violence and invasion was through prayer and providing support for the Church.

Across the Channel, Viking settlers had taken control of Normandy (Norman meant 'North-man': Vikings from the north). By 1060, these Viking settlers had become very like their French neighbours, but they still had strong links with Scandinavia, allowing Viking raiders to take shelter in their harbours and ports. They also remained a powerful military threat.

Learning outcomes

In this chapter you will find out:

- how Anglo-Saxon society worked
- how Harold Godwinson became king of England
- why other people also claimed the throne of England
- what happened in 1066: the year of the Norman invasion.

1.1 Anglo-Saxon society

Learning outcomes

- Understand the Anglo-Saxon social system and the power of the monarch.
- Understand how England was governed and the role of the Church.
- Understand the economy of Anglo-Saxon England.

What was England like in 1060? Compared to now, there were very few people: about two million in the whole of England – less than half the population of London today. Life was hard and life expectancy was low because of high rates of infant mortality. Almost everyone farmed land in order to grow what they needed to live on. Right at the top of Anglo-Saxon* society were the aristocracy* – the social elite. Right at the bottom of Anglo-Saxon society were the slaves.

Key terms

Anglo-Saxon*

People who had settled in England after the Romans left Britain. They came from different parts of what is now Germany, Belgium and the Netherlands.

Aristocracy*

The people in society who are seen as being important because of their wealth and power, which they have often inherited from their parents and ancestors.

The social system

Peasant farmers

The majority of Anglo-Saxons were peasant farmers, who rented small farms that they worked for themselves and their families. Peasants did a set amount of work for the local lord as well as working the land to support themselves and their families. If they did not carry out this work for their lord then the peasants could lose their right to use the land.

There was also a group of peasants called ceorls* who were free to go and work for another lord if they wanted to. These ceorls still had to carry out some services for their local lord in return for the right to farm the land. No one used land without carrying out some kind of service to someone else.

Key term

Ceorls*

'Free' peasant farmers not tied to their land.

Slaves

10% of the Anglo-Saxon population were slaves. Slaves could be bought and sold. If they committed crimes, they were often not punished as harshly as other people because it might damage their ability to work: they were seen more like property than people. The Normans thought that owning slaves was barbaric, but it was a normal part of Anglo-Saxon society.

Thegns

Thegns were the local lords. There were between 4,000 and 5,000 thegns by 1060. A thegn was an important man in the local community: holding more land than the peasants (more than five hides* of land), and living in a manor house with a tower and a separate church. Thegns were the aristocracy of the Anglo-Saxon age, its warrior class.

Key term

Hides*

The measurement used for land in Anglo-Saxon and Norman England. One hide was about 120 acres: the amount a family needed to support themselves.

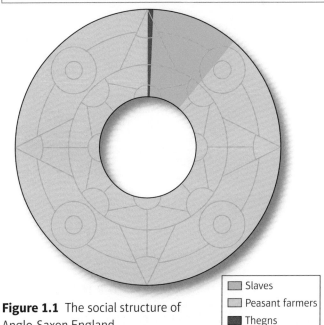

Figure 1.1 The social structure of Anglo-Saxon England.

- Slaves
- Peasant farmers
- Thegns

Thegns

Thegns were divided into king's thegns, who held their land direct from the king and served him directly, and those who held their land from earls and other thegns.

When a man became a thegn, he paid a tax called a heriot. Heriot meant 'war gear' and the tax required a thegn to equip himself with a helmet and coat of mail, a horse and harness, and a sword and spear.

Earls

Earls* were the most important aristocrats: the most important men in the country after the king. The relationship between the king and his earls was based on loyalty. The earls competed against each other to be the one the king trusted and relied on the most, so that the king would give them the greatest rewards and honour. Sometimes, earls even challenged the king to get more power.

Figure 1.2 The main earldoms of England in 1060.

Earls*

Highest Anglo-Saxon aristocracy. The word came from the Danish 'jarl' and meant a chieftain who ruled a region on behalf of the king. The area controlled by an earl is called an earldom.

Changing social status

In other parts of Europe, such as in Normandy, people's status in society depended on ancestry: the importance of their family and ancestors. Anglo-Saxon society was much less rigid than this.

- A peasant who prospered and obtained five hides of land that he paid tax on could gain the status of a thegn.
- Merchants who made a number of trips abroad in their own ships could also become thegns.
- Slaves could be freed by their masters and free peasants could sell themselves into slavery as a desperate measure to feed their families.
- At the top of the social system, thegns could be raised to the status of earls (and earls could be demoted to thegns). Earls could sometimes even become kings.

Describe **two** features of the social system of Anglo-Saxon England. **4 marks**

This question is about identifying key features. You need to identify two relevant points and then develop each point. For example: 'The social system was not fixed. This meant a free peasant who did very well could become a thegn.'

Anglo-Saxon England

The areas of Britain controlled by Anglo-Saxons had changed over the centuries. Viking invasions had taken control of vast areas, which had then been recaptured. Anglo-Saxon England also had hostile neighbours: Wales, Scotland and Ireland and, to the south, Normandy. The location of Normandy is included on this map, but it was never under Anglo-Saxon control.

The power of the English monarchy

In 1060, the king (monarch) was Edward the Confessor. He was the most powerful person in Anglo-Saxon England. He governed the country.

Powers of the king	Duties of the people
Law-making: the king created new laws and made sure they were enforced throughout the country.	To obey the law as it was passed down through the king's local representatives.
Money: the king controlled the production of the silver pennies used as money.	To use the king's coins. Forging coins was a very serious crime.
Landownership: the king owned large estates and could grant land out to his followers. He could also take land away from those who had acted against him.	Land carried with it obligations to the king. The main two obligations were payment of tax and military service.
Military power: the king had the ability to raise a national army and fleet.	Landholders had to provide and equip fighters for the army or fleet; otherwise they were fined or lost their land.
Taxation: the king decided when taxes should be paid and a national taxation system delivered this tax to him.	Landholders had to pay their taxes, otherwise they were fined or lost their land.

Figure 1.3 The powers of Edward the Confessor and the duties of his people. The image in the middle is a representation of Edward's royal seal. This was attached to his royal orders to show they came from the king.

The king's role was to protect his people from attack and give them laws to maintain safety and security at home. In return, the people of England owed him service. Every boy swore an oath* when they reached 12 years of age to be faithful to the king. The oath was administered by the shire reeve* at a special ceremony held each year (see Source A).

Source A

The oath sworn by Anglo-Saxon boys once they reached 12 years of age.

All shall swear in the name of the Lord, before whom every holy thing is holy, that they will be faithful to the king. ... From the day on which this oath shall be rendered, no one shall conceal the breach of it on the part of a brother or family relation, any more than in a stranger.

How powerful was Edward the Confessor?

Kings of Anglo-Saxon England held their power ultimately because they led armies. Anglo-Saxon kings had clawed England back from Viking control. Edward the Confessor was not a warrior king, but his earls and their thegns were a powerful military force and he relied on his earls, especially Earl Godwin, to protect England from attack.

Kings who were war leaders gained legitimacy for their rule because they could hand out the wealth and land of their defeated enemies to their followers. When kings did not have success in battle then their power could be reduced. However, Edward had other reasons that made him a legitimate king.

Key terms

Oath*

A solemn promise to do something. Anglo-Saxons swore oaths on holy relics to make them especially binding. A relic was often a body part of a dead saint, kept in a special casket.

Shire reeve*

An official of the king: his sheriff. Sheriffs managed the king's estates, collected revenue for him and were in charge of local courts.

- **He was a respected law-maker.** Anglo-Saxon society as a whole valued kings who kept things peaceful, because quarrels between families were common and could frequently break out into fighting that threatened everyone in a community.

- **He was pious (very religious).** Anglo-Saxon kings claimed a special link to God: they were anointed* as a representative of Christ on Earth. It was believed that a worthy king could bring God's blessing to his country and that God could also guide his actions.

Key term

Anointed*

To put sacred oil on someone as part of a religious ceremony.

Limits to the king's power

Anglo-Saxon kings needed to rule the whole of England, but half the country, called the Danelaw*, was Anglo-Danish. Many of its inhabitants were the descendants of Viking invaders. Although they accepted Edward's rule, people wanted to be ruled by local men and to follow their own laws and customs.

While the Danelaw area represented an administrative challenge, Edward the Confessor's real problems were with Earl Godwin of Wessex. Wessex was the richest earldom of England and Godwin and his family owned so much land that they were as rich as the king. They were lords to so many thegns that they were militarily much more powerful than the king. While Anglo-Saxon society viewed disloyalty to your lord as the ultimate crime, there was no reason why Godwin should not try to put pressure on the king to do things his way. For example, to appoint some of Godwin's men to important Church positions or give earldoms to his sons.

Tensions between Godwin and Edward had come to a head in 1050. The king had ordered Godwin to punish the people of Dover after a visiting embassy* from Boulogne was attacked. Godwin had refused. As a result, Edward, with the help of two other important earls, Siward of Northumbria and Leofric of Mercia, forced Godwin into exile. But, in 1051, Godwin returned with a fleet and an army. He asked Edward if his earldom could be restored to him. To prevent war, Edward agreed.

Activities ?

1 While you are at school, your teacher (your lord) provides you with education and looks after your well-being. What duties do you owe your teacher in return?

2 Describe two features of Anglo-Saxon monarchy that enabled the king to protect England from foreign invasions.

3 Explain two ways in which 'over-mighty' earls, like Earl Godwin, could challenge the king's power. Use the example of Godwin's refusal to punish those responsible for the fight in Dover to help you make a convincing argument.

Key terms

The Danelaw*

The part of England where Danish (Viking) power had been strongest and which had kept some of its Danish laws instead of Anglo-Saxon ones. You can see the area occupied by the Danelaw in Figure 1.2.

Embassy*

An official visit by representatives of one ruler to another ruler.

Government

The Witan

The Witan was a council that advised the king on issues of government. It was made up of the most important aristocrats of the kingdom, including earls and archbishops. It discussed:

- possible threats from foreign powers
- religious affairs
- land disputes and how to settle them.

The Witan also had an important role in approving a new king, which will be looked at later (page 28).

The king did not have to follow the Witan's advice. The king also decided who was appointed to the Witan and when it was to meet.

Source B

The king and his Witan. This image is from an 11th-century book of Old Testament Bible stories. It is useful for historians of Anglo-Saxon England because the artists have portrayed the Old Testament king as though he was an Anglo-Saxon king, surrounded by his advisers.

Earldoms

What power did earls have?

Earldoms had been introduced by the Viking king of England, Cnut, after he had invaded and conquered Anglo-Saxon England in 1015. At first, Cnut made his followers the earls of four great earldoms, but he soon passed the title on to the leader of the most important family in each earldom. For example, Cnut made Godwin Earl of Wessex in the 1030s. Godwin was not a Dane, like Cnut – he was an Anglo-Saxon thegn from Sussex. However, Godwin had shown he was a man that Cnut could trust to follow him loyally.

In order to aid the king in governing the country, the earls were given many of the powers of the king.

- They were responsible for collecting the taxes of their earldom and they received a share of all the revenue collected. This share was very large – a third – and it meant that earls were rich. They were supposed to use this economic power to ensure their earldom was well defended and well run.

- They oversaw justice and legal punishments in their earldom. Most types of crime came under their jurisdiction (the things they were responsible for), although only the king could make new laws. This gave the earls strong social powers: controlling and influencing the way people lived.

- They had great military power. They were the lords to many hundreds of thegns, and also maintained an elite bodyguard of professional soldiers called housecarls*. The king therefore used his earls like generals: they were his military leaders against the king's enemies.

These powers gave the earls economic, legal and military control of their earldoms. The big earldoms (see Figure 1.2) formed enormous 'power bases' for their earls.

Key term

Housecarls*

Highly-trained troops that stayed with their lord wherever he went; a bodyguard.

13

Limits to the earls' powers

When a king was strong, as Cnut was for most of his reign, the power of the earls was definitely less than that of the king. A powerful king like Cnut would demand obedience and would punish those who failed him. But a king like Edward the Confessor was not so strong. He had spent most of his life in exile and did not have the backing of hundreds of important followers in England. It seems likely that he had to depend on Earl Godwin in particular. When Edward brought Normans into important positions in English government, Godwin and the other earls resisted their appointments and worked to get the Normans sent home again (see page 21).

However, the earls' power relied on the support of the thegns in their earldoms. We know this because of occasions when thegns demanded that earls be removed from their positions. This happened in 1065 when Earl Tostig, the son of Godwin, lost his earldom and went into exile after protests from his thegns about the way he governed his earldom, Northumbria.

Extend your knowledge

Earl Tostig

Tostig Godwinson was made Earl of Northumbria, a huge earldom, in 1055. Tostig was earl for ten years and he took his responsibility to keep law and order very seriously. Northumbria was plagued by bandits, who laid in wait for travellers and robbed them, often killing their victims. Tostig ordered that all such men be hunted down and either killed (if they were ordinary people) or mutilated (if they were from important families). This decisive action meant that people were soon able to travel safely again, until Tostig was exiled in 1065 and law and order broke down once more.

However, Tostig did not only use his powers to make his earldom safer for travellers. He also used them to benefit himself. He did this by warning rich families that they would be accused of being bandits unless they paid him money.

Tostig's example shows that the powers of the earl could be very useful for saving major problems in an earldom, but they could also prove a threat to good government if they were misused.

Local government

The shire, the hundred and the hide

Earldoms were divided into shires. Shires had social, political, economic and military functions.

- **Social:** each shire had its own court for trying cases and giving punishments.
- **Political:** the shire reeve acted as the king's representative in the shire (see next page).
- **Economic:** each shire had a burh (fortified town) as its main administrative and trading centre.
- **Military:** each shire provided troops for the fyrd* (see below).

Shires were divided into **hundreds***, and hundreds into **tithings*** – units of ten households. At the base of the whole administrative system was the hide. Each hide of land carried obligations: payment of taxes and military service.

Key terms

Fyrd*

The men of the Anglo-Saxon army and fleet. Every five hides provided one man for the fyrd.

Hundreds*

A unit of land administration. In some parts of England, a hundred was 100 hides of land, but in other areas it didn't have this direct connection.

Tithings*

An administrative unit that was a group of ten households – originally equivalent to a tenth of a hundred in some areas.

Exam-style question, Section B

Describe **two** features of earldoms in Anglo-Saxon England.   **4 marks**

Exam tip

A feature is something that is distinctive or characteristic – we distinguish one person from another, for example, by recognising their distinctive facial features. So, when a question asks for two features of earldoms, think about the things that made earldoms distinctive – their special characteristics. Remember to develop each point to explain the feature.

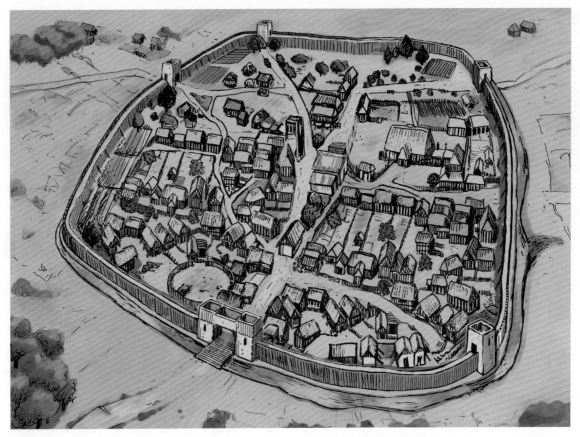

Figure 1.4 Artist's impression of an Anglo-Saxon burh. Strong walls enclose the whole town and everyone who lived in the burh shared responsibilities for maintaining the defences.

Shire reeves

The shire reeves, or sheriffs, were the king's local government officials and they worked within the earldoms to look after the king's interests and carry out his instructions. Their duties included:

- collecting revenues from the king's land
- collecting the geld tax*
- collecting fines from the shire court
- enforcing and witnessing the law at the shire court
- responsibilities for providing men for the fyrd and for the upkeep of roads and fortifications.

The king issued his orders to the shire reeves through writs. These were written instructions with a seal stamped by the king.

> **Key term**
>
> **Geld tax***
>
> A tax on land, originally to pay off the Vikings (Danegeld). It went to the king.

Military service – the fyrd

When the call came from the king, each group of five hides was obliged to provide one man for the fyrd, together with his battle equipment. Some historians argue that there were two types of fyrd:

- The **select** fyrd gathered men to fight anywhere in England for the king.
- The **general** fyrd gathered men to fight who didn't travel outside their local area.

The select fyrd was made up of thegns and their followers, rather than the general populace. The thegns probably trained together and were well-equipped with weapons, armour and horses. However, these men could only stay away from home for so long before the management of their farms would suffer – especially at harvest time, when lots of people were needed to cut the crops and bring them into storage. A period of 40 days was therefore fixed for their service, after which a fyrd would be disbanded.

The legal system

The king and the law

The king was the law-maker, issuing laws to fulfil his role of keeping the peace. Offences against the king's peace, such as robbing a traveller, were punished harshly. The people of England looked to the king to provide peace. The people also expected the king to provide justice: to treat everyone of the same social standing in the same way.

Blood feuds and Wergild

Traditionally, if a family member was attacked, then the rest of the family would find the person responsible and punish them. This led to blood feuds*. Feuds could continue for generations and they could spread to affect whole communities.

The solution to the blood feud problem was Wergild. Instead of taking revenge, the family who had suffered the murder were paid compensation by the murderer's family. The Wergild system showed a commitment to fairness in Anglo-Saxon society as it gave equal status to all people of a certain social standing. However, it also shows the importance of status.

- A ceorl was worth 20 shillings.
- A thegn was worth 1,200 shillings.
- An earl or an archbishop was worth 3,600 shillings.

It is difficult to make direct comparisons with our money today, but some historians suggest 1 shilling was equivalent to £100 today.

Key term

Blood feuds*

A revenge system based on family loyalties and honour. If someone was killed, the victim's family had the right to kill someone from the murderer's family, who then had the right to revenge themselves, and so on.

Collective responsibility

When a crime was committed, it was the duty of all members of a tithing to hunt for the criminal: this was called the 'hue and cry'. The men of the tithing were also responsible for the good behaviour of their ten households. If someone was proved to have done something wrong, they had to pay a fine. If, for example, someone from their village refused to join the general fyrd, there would be consequences for everyone in the tithing. This community-based justice system followed a principle called 'collective responsibility'.

Activities ?

1 Imagine that your class is divided into groups of ten and that you are collectively responsible for each other's behaviour. What are the advantages of this system for your teacher and the school? Are there any disadvantages to the system?

2 Come up with one strength and one weakness of the fyrd system for defending Anglo-Saxon England from attack.

3 Describe how each of the following was involved in the government of Anglo-Saxon England. Which one was most important, in your view? Explain your answer.

  a Earls   **c** Geld tax

  b Shire reeves   **d** The Witan

The Anglo-Saxon economy

Historians are not entirely sure about what England produced that enabled it to trade so effectively; wool and cloth products are likely to have been the most important products because we know they were vital to English trade later in the medieval period. Western England was particularly well-suited to sheep rearing. Eastern England had drier conditions and fertile soils that made it excellent for arable farming (growing crops). Farming was well-organised: for example, there were over 6,000 mills throughout the country used for grinding the local community's grain into flour.

Most of the silver used to make Anglo-Saxon coins came from Germany, rather than being mined in Britain. Silver was very valuable, so England must have been able to export products that had high value abroad to be able to import silver from Germany.

There is also evidence of other products from Europe being used in Anglo-Saxon England, including millstones (used in Anglo-Saxon mills) and whetstones (used to sharpen blades) from Denmark, and wine from Normandy.

Source C

An Anglo-Saxon silver penny from Edward the Confessor's reign. The coin shows Edward sitting on his throne. He is holding an orb (the ball-shaped object) and a sceptre: symbols of royalty that are still used by the British monarchy today.

Extend your knowledge

Making coins

The king controlled the process of minting (making) coins. Coins had to be a standard thickness and weight. The metal stamps that were used to make the coins were issued from a central location controlled by the king. There were harsh punishments for any forging.

Towns

By the end of Edward's reign in 1066, something like 10% of the population of England lived in towns. Each shire had its main town. These fortified burhs had been planned so that no one was more than 15 or 20 miles from safety if news of a Viking raiding party reached them. They were linked by roads so that troops could move quickly from one burh to another.

They had strong walls and ramparts (steep earth banks) guarded by men from the town (see Figure 1.4). Administration and upkeep of the town and its fortifications was the responsibility of the burh's inhabitants.

Towns and trade

The burhs were also trading hubs. The king's laws demanded that all trade worth more than a set amount of money should take place in a burh, so that trade tax could be paid. By 1060, London and York were the biggest cities in England, with populations of more than 10,000 people. Towns like Norwich and Lincoln had populations of around 6,000.

Towns often grew in importance because of international trading links. York was a centre for trade with Denmark, for example; Bristol was the centre of trade between the west of England and Viking settlements in southern Ireland. London was probably the biggest trading hub of all, with documents from the time listing the presence in London of traders from Germany, France, Normandy and Flanders. These traders would have taken back reports about England to their own countries.

Villages

Historians think that many of the villages in England today began in Anglo-Saxon times, but not as a cluster of houses grouped around a church, surrounded by the village's fields. Villages were more likely to be a large number of quite isolated homes and farms scattered over the countryside. The houses were made of wood and thatched with straw, and were homes for lots of relatives living together rather than just one family. Most thegns lived in the countryside too. Their manor houses were larger and better built than peasant huts. Some of these manor houses may have been fortified against attack. Thegns often built a church on their land, too, and employed a priest to hold services for the thegn's household. These churches would also provide services for the surrounding area. It was connections to the local thegn and to the local church that brought people together into a village.

The influence of the Church

There were many reforms to Church teachings and practice happening in Europe by 1060 but, unlike in Normandy, English bishops were not very involved in these changes. The English Church was traditionally-minded, resistant to reform, and it focused on Anglo-Saxon saints as well as older Celtic saints. These Anglo-Saxon and Celtic saints were often linked to a local area and were saints that the local people felt were familiar: part of their everyday lives.

The Church was organised into large areas, each controlled by a bishop. The bishops were often rich, important people. Bishops served on the Witan as the king's advisers. Norman sources paint some English bishops as being corrupt: selling Church jobs for profit, though this may have been unfair in some cases. There was a tension between bishops and the churches set up by thegns: bishops did not want local priests being hired and fired by anyone else except them. Gradually, these local priests and their parishes were brought under the bishops' control.

Local priests were usually quite ordinary members of the community. They were not especially well-educated (many could not read Latin, the language of the Church), they had small landholdings like peasants and they were usually married, which went against the reforms that required priests to be celibate (single, and not involved in sexual relationships).

England also had monasteries and nunneries: religious communities of monks and nuns headed by abbots and abbesses. Unlike in Normandy, monasteries were in decline. Numbers were shrinking and, in the monasteries that survived, monks formed part of their local communities rather than living separate, holy lives apart from the world.

Religion in Anglo-Saxon England was an important part of everyday life. The influence of the Church was very strong because people were worried about what would happen when they died. Everyone believed that they would spend time in the afterlife being punished for their sins, and participating in religious activity and prayer provided a way for people to reduce this period of punishment.

Religion was important to King Edward, who devoted much of his later years to rebuilding Westminster cathedral, and also to people's idea of what a king should be. The king was an agent of God, and his conduct and rule had to reflect this. Contemporary sources show that English people believed God would be quick to punish countries for the sinful behaviour of their people, especially sinfulness within the Church or monarchy.

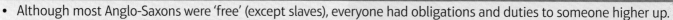

Summary

- Although most Anglo-Saxons were 'free' (except slaves), everyone had obligations and duties to someone higher up.
- The king was very powerful and made the laws governing England.
- Local government and local justice was administered by local people and officials.
- England had a strong economy and an effective tax system.

Checkpoint

Strengthen

S1 Describe the differences between slaves, ceorls (free farmers), thegns and earls.

S2 Write a paragraph on 'a day in the life of a shire reeve'. Think about the duties that they were expected to perform.

S3 Explain what each of the following was: geld tax, the fyrd, a burh.

Challenge

C1 Summarise three ways in which the Anglo-Saxon king was more powerful than his earls.

C2 Explain why thegns were important in Anglo-Saxon England.

How confident do you feel about your answers to these questions? If you are not sure that you have answered them well, try the following study skills activity.

Activity ?

Focused listing is a useful study skill to develop. Here's how it works:

a Write out the main Topic headings, e.g. Anglo-Saxon society, The power of the monarchy, Government, etc.

b For each one, read quickly through the text and then close the book.

c Then, for each heading, make a list of the main terms and ideas you can recall about it.

d Check back through the book to see what you left out.

Use this method to make notes on the 'Government' and 'Economy' of Anglo-Saxon England sections.

1.2 The last years of Edward the Confessor and the succession crisis

Timeline

The last years of Edward the Confessor

1053 Death of Earl Godwin; Harold Godwinson becomes Earl of Wessex

1055 Tostig Godwinson made Earl of Northumbria

1062 The Godwins defeat the Welsh king, Gruffudd ap Llywelyn

1064 Harold's embassy to Normandy

1065 Uprising against Earl Tostig; Tostig exiled

1066 Death of Edward the Confessor; Harold becomes king

The house of Godwin

The house of Godwin* began in 1018 during King Cnut's reign, when Cnut made his favourite adviser, Godwin, Earl of Wessex. Godwin was probably the son of an Anglo-Saxon thegn.

Key term

House of Godwin*

The 'house' of Godwin refers to the Godwin family. The current British royal family is the house of Windsor, for example.

Extend your knowledge

King Cnut

Cnut was king of England from 1016 to 1035. When he took control of England, he executed leading Anglo-Saxons who might have led rebellions against his rule. Then he began to promote Anglo-Saxons he could trust alongside his Danish followers.

Political power in Anglo-Saxon England had strong family connections. Godwin had helped Edward the Confessor to become king and, in return, the king married Godwin's daughter, Edith of Wessex, in 1045. That family link to the throne was very significant in Anglo-Saxon society. Brothers-in-laws of kings had succeeded to the throne in the past.

Harold's succession as Earl of Wessex

When Godwin died in 1053, his family's influence was reduced as rival earls jostled for position. However, the Godwins built up their control again. By the mid-1060s the Godwins had control of almost all England.

- Harold Godwinson succeeded his father as Earl of Wessex, giving him riches, influence over hundreds of thegns and a powerful position as adviser to the king.
- In 1055, Tostig Godwinson (Harold's brother) became the new Earl of Northumbria. That gave the Godwins a powerbase in the far north of England.
- In 1057, the earldom of East Anglia was given to Gyrth Godwinson, Harold's teenage brother.
- Also in 1057, a smaller earldom in the south-west Midlands went to Leofwine Godwinson – another younger brother of Harold.

Why did Edward the Confessor allow the Godwins to increase their power so extensively?

- Edward's marriage to Edith was certainly important, making him kin to the Godwins.
- England was under threat from Norway, meaning that Edward needed his earls to be strong military leaders. That is probably the reason why Tostig was made Earl of Northumbria instead of the old earl's son, Waltheof, who was too young to lead men into battle.
- Harold's marriage to Edith the Fair (another Edith) may also have influenced the Godwins' gaining East Anglia, as she is thought to have inherited large estates in that region.

Military success

The only significant rival to the Godwins left in England by the 1060s was Aelfgar, Earl of Mercia. He was exiled twice in the 1050s, teaming up with the Welsh king, Gruffudd ap Llywelyn, both times to fight for the return of his earldom. When Aelfgar died, probably in 1062, King Edward and the Godwins acted swiftly. They didn't want Llywelyn working with rivals again to challenge their interests. After a surprise attack in 1062, which Llywelyn escaped, Harold took a fleet round the coast of South Wales while Tostig led an army overland into North Wales.

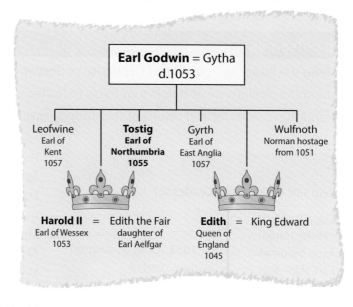

Earl Godwin = Gytha
d.1053

Leofwine
Earl of Kent
1057

Tostig
Earl of Northumbria
1055

Gyrth
Earl of East Anglia
1057

Wulfnoth
Norman hostage from 1051

Harold II = Edith the Fair
Earl of Wessex   daughter of
1053   Earl Aelfgar

Edith = King Edward
Queen of England
1045

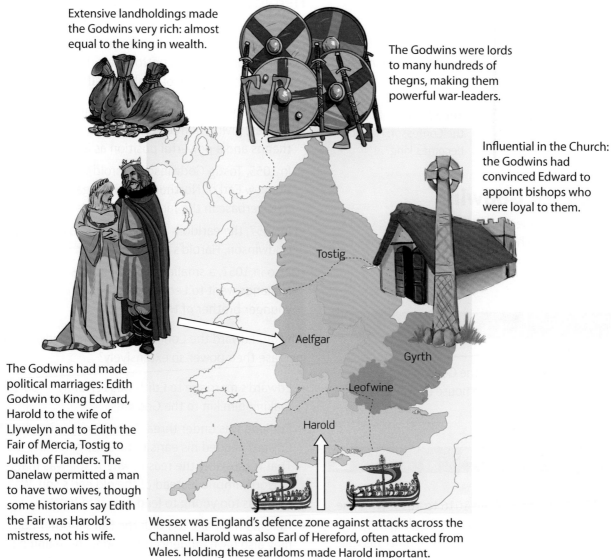

Extensive landholdings made the Godwins very rich: almost equal to the king in wealth.

The Godwins were lords to many hundreds of thegns, making them powerful war-leaders.

Influential in the Church: the Godwins had convinced Edward to appoint bishops who were loyal to them.

The Godwins had made political marriages: Edith Godwin to King Edward, Harold to the wife of Llywelyn and to Edith the Fair of Mercia, Tostig to Judith of Flanders. The Danelaw permitted a man to have two wives, though some historians say Edith the Fair was Harold's mistress, not his wife.

Tostig

Aelfgar

Gyrth

Leofwine

Harold

Wessex was England's defence zone against attacks across the Channel. Harold was also Earl of Hereford, often attacked from Wales. Holding these earldoms made Harold important.

Figure 1.5 The power of the Godwins in 1060.

Their joint strategy was a brilliant success. Harold sent Llywelyn's head to Edward the Confessor, but it was Harold himself who appointed a new 'puppet' king for Wales whom he could control. Harold had assumed the role of *sub regulus* – the king's deputy, leader of his armies: by far the most powerful of Edward's earls.

Godwin and the king

Edward showed signs earlier in his reign of trying to shake off Godwin's control. In 1042, he had appointed some Normans to influential positions, causing conflict with aristocrats like Godwin. Norman sources insist that Edward promised the English throne to William of Normandy after his death, in return for William's support against Godwin. What's not clear, however, is what help, if any, was given from Normandy: Godwin was returned to power in 1051 without any intervention from Normandy, and his sons were given the most powerful positions in the kingdom.

Extend your knowledge

Edward and Normandy

What we know of as France today was not the same in 1060. Normandy, part of France today, was then an independent dukedom. The duke of Normandy owed duty to the king of France, but that did not stop regular wars between them, or between Normandy and other counties such as Flanders, Boulogne and Brittany. In fact, Normandy had once been part of Brittany.

Edward the Confessor had a close relationship with Normandy. Edward's mother, Emma, was from Normandy and, when Vikings seized the throne of England, Edward went into exile there in 1016. He lived there for 25 years.

When Edward became king of England in 1043, he brought with him favourites of his from Normandy. Anglo-Saxon England and Normandy were very well connected by 1060.

Activities ?

1. Identify one way in which the Godwins were economically powerful, one way in which they were militarily powerful and one way in which they were politically powerful.

2. Give three pieces of evidence (or extra information) to explain each of the three choices you made in question 1.

3. Edward the Confessor was 57 in 1060: an old man in Anglo-Saxon times. To what extent do you think the Godwins became so powerful because Edward was not strong enough to control them? Or, do you think the Godwins helped Edward to rule England successfully? Write up your answer after discussing it with a partner. Make sure you back up your points with evidence and reach a decision on these questions at the end of your answer.

Harold's embassy to Normandy

Harold Godwinson went to Normandy in the early summer of 1064 (or possibly 1065) on a mission for King Edward – a type of visit called an embassy.

Harold travelled to France, but landed in Ponthieu, a small county between Normandy and Flanders – perhaps blown off-course by a storm. Harold was taken prisoner by Count Guy of Ponthieu, but Duke William heard of the capture and demanded that Guy hand Harold over. Harold then spent time with William in Normandy, and helped him in two military campaigns, which resulted in William giving Harold gifts of weapons and armour. These gifts were symbolic of the relationship between a lord and his warrior.

After relaying King Edward's message to William (it's unknown what that message was), Harold made a solemn oath to William, swearing on two holy relics. This could have been an oath of allegiance: Harold swearing to support William's claim to the throne of England.

Anglo-Saxon and Norman interpretations of why he went on this mission differ.

- The Norman interpretation of the visit was that King Edward commissioned Harold to go to talk to Duke William about plans for William's succession, and that the visit involved Harold swearing allegiance to him as his future king.
- The Anglo-Saxon interpretation is that Harold went to recover two hostages* from William – Harold's brother and his nephew, Wulfnoth and Hakon.

Key term

Hostages*

People given to another as part of an oath or agreement. If the oath or agreement was broken, the hostages could be killed or maimed [e.g. have hands cut off, be blinded (or both)].

Harold's embassy to Normandy is difficult to interpret, but it is significant in three main ways:

- It shows that Harold was King Edward's trusted adviser, as this was clearly an important embassy, whatever its overall aim actually was.
- It was used by the Normans to boost William's claim to the throne. Even if the embassy was not about William becoming king of England, it suggests close ties between England and Normandy.
- It was used by the Normans to portray Harold as an oath-breaker after Harold became king instead of helping William to the throne of England. Even if Harold never actually swore allegiance to William, it is a useful indication of how important such oaths of allegiance between a lord and a follower were in both Anglo-Saxon and Norman society.

Source A

A scene from the Bayeux Tapestry, probably produced in Kent around 1070 on the orders of Bishop Odo of Bayeux. This scene shows Harold swearing an oath in William's presence.

The rising against Earl Tostig

Reasons for the rising

Tostig Godwinson became Earl of Northumbria in 1055 after the death of Earl Siward. Northumbria was an important earldom because it was very large (see Figure 1.5), it guarded the border with Scotland and had a long history of Viking attacks and settlement. Because it had a long association with the Vikings, and was a long way away from the powerbase of the Anglo-Saxon king in the south, it was the obvious entry point for further Viking invasions.

Northumbria was very different from Wessex, the richest of all the earldoms and the Godwins' powerbase in the south of England. Much of it was part of the Danelaw, the area that had been settled by the Vikings. There were some different laws and customs, hence 'Dane-law'. People in the Danelaw used lots of words borrowed from the Scandinavian languages of the Vikings. It is probable that a southerner, like Tostig, would have found understanding the Northumbrians difficult.

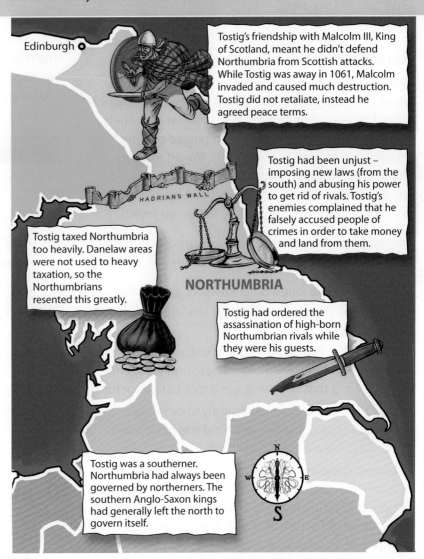

Tostig's friendship with Malcolm III, King of Scotland, meant he didn't defend Northumbria from Scottish attacks. While Tostig was away in 1061, Malcolm invaded and caused much destruction. Tostig did not retaliate, instead he agreed peace terms.

Tostig had been unjust – imposing new laws (from the south) and abusing his power to get rid of rivals. Tostig's enemies complained that he falsely accused people of crimes in order to take money and land from them.

Tostig taxed Northumbria too heavily. Danelaw areas were not used to heavy taxation, so the Northumbrians resented this greatly.

Tostig had ordered the assassination of high-born Northumbrian rivals while they were his guests.

Tostig was a southerner. Northumbria had always been governed by northerners. The southern Anglo-Saxon kings had generally left the north to govern itself.

Earl Tostig ruled Northumbria for ten years. In October 1065, there was an uprising against Tostig, led by important Northumbrian thegns. There were several reasons for the rising, as illustrated on the right.

Extend your knowledge

Danelaw differences

Danelaw differences were often more about similar things being called something different, for example the hundred was called the *wapentake* and a hide was called a *carucate* in the Danelaw.

Other differences were more significant. There were many more ceorls in the Danelaw part of England: peasants who were not bound in service to their lord and who could, if they wanted to, go and work for someone else. Also, because the geld tax had originally been used to pay Vikings not to attack England, the northern Danegeld regions paid taxes at a much lower rate than other parts of the country.

Extend your knowledge

Northumbrian resentment

The resentment against Tostig had been building over many years, with most of the reasons for the rising being long-term ones: over-taxation and unfairness. The trigger for the rising in 1065 was Tostig's murder (in 1064) of two followers of Gospatric (a leading Northumbrian aristocrat) after Tostig had invited them to York. Soon after, Gospatric was himself assassinated after he had travelled south to King Edward's court to complain about Tostig to the king. This was viewed in Northumbria as the very worst kind of treachery.

The rising of 1065 began with rebels marching on York, the city from which Northumbria was governed. There, the rebels killed as many of Tostig's housecarls and servants as they could find, and declared Tostig an outlaw. They invited Morcar, the brother of the Earl of Mercia, to be their earl instead of Tostig.

Harold's response to the rising

King Edward held a conference to decide what to do about the rising. The outcome was surprising. Instead of raising an army to march north and defeat the rebels, Harold instead met with them and passed on King Edward's agreement to their terms. Harold married Morcar's sister (his second wife) and was given large landholdings in Mercia. The rising had begun at the start of October 1065. By 1 November, Tostig was exiled.

There are not enough sources to be sure exactly what happened, but the evidence seems to suggest that:

- Harold, like the king's other advisers, agreed that Tostig had pushed Northumbria too far: Tostig was to blame for the rising.
- Furious that Harold had not backed him, Tostig angrily accused Harold of having conspired against him, saying that the rising was a plot to replace him.
- King Edward commanded an army to be raised to put down the rising, but his command was not obeyed. Harold made excuses and the other earls did the same.
- Edward therefore had no choice but to accept the rebels' demands. Their choice of Morcar was diplomatic – another southerner, like Edward himself, when the rebels could have pushed for a Northumbrian, such as Waltheof, the son of their old earl, Siward.

Why would Harold have acted to weaken the house of Godwin and betray his brother? It is likely that Harold's ambitions were now greater than the interests of his family: he wanted to be king.

- Edward the Confessor was old and ill (he died three months after the Northumbrian rising).
- Harold needed a united kingdom to hold off the threats from Normandy and Scandinavia: a war with Mercia and Northumbria would weaken English defences.
- Tostig was a rival to the throne. Although his exile and enmity was probably something Harold regretted, it must have seemed a lesser evil than allowing him to challenge his ambition.

The powers of the king – revisited

It was very significant that the earls, led by Harold, failed to obey King Edward's command. Earls were bound by oaths of loyalty to their king and they were supposed to act as his military leaders.

The refusal to lead an army against the rebels therefore shows that the power of the king could sometimes be challenged: if the king was weak and if it was in the interests of all the major earls to act together.

Exam-style question, Section B ○

Explain why there was a rising against Earl Tostig in 1065.

You may use the following in your answer:

- the Danelaw
- taxation.

You **must** also use information of your own. **12 marks**

Exam tip ○

'Explain why' questions require you to identify relevant points that you can link together to construct a convincing explanation. Take care not simply to tell the story of the rebellion, which would be description. Instead, link each point you make to the question through analysis.

Death of Edward the Confessor

Edward the Confessor had no children with his wife, Edith of Wessex, daughter of Earl Godwin. This meant that, when he died on 5 January 1066, there was a succession* crisis.

Key term

Succession* (to the throne)

The process that decides who should be the next king or queen and 'succeed' to the throne.

The Bayeux Tapestry shows the death of Edward at his palace in Westminster – a picture of this scene is on the next page. Edward is with a small circle of people: his wife Edith, who sits at his feet; Stigand, the Anglo-Saxon Archbishop of Canterbury; one of Edward's ministers and Harold. Edward is shown holding out his hand to Harold. Other sources report that Edward said to Harold: 'I commend this woman [Edith] with all the kingdom to your protection.' Harold understood this to mean that he was to be king – Harold II. However, there were others who thought they had better claims to the throne: a situation that made the year 1066 a very eventful one!

Source B

The death of Edward the Confessor, portrayed in the Bayeux Tapestry.

Summary

- The house of Godwin had become the real 'power behind the throne' in Anglo-Saxon England.
- Harold's embassy to Normandy and his decisions over Tostig had major consequences.
- Edward the Confessor died childless, causing a succession crisis.

Checkpoint

Strengthen

S1 When did: Harold become Earl of Wessex; Tostig get exiled; King Edward die?

S2 Describe two aspects of the house of Godwin that made them so powerful.

Challenge

C1 In your own words, summarise three reasons why you think Harold went against King Edward's wishes over the rising against Tostig.

C2 What else would it be useful to know about the consequences of Tostig's exile?

How confident do you feel about your answers to these questions? If you are not sure that you have answered them well, try the following study skills activity.

Activity ?

KWL is a strategy to help you take control of your own learning. It stands for Know – Want to know – Learned. This is how it works:

a Draw a table with three columns: 'Know', 'Want to know' and 'Learned'.

b For any topic you are learning about, write down what you know about it already.

c Next, write down what else you'd like know, what questions you have about what you know.

d When you find out the answers, write them in the 'Learned' column.

Use this method to make notes on this section. Here's an example:

Know	Want to know	Learned
Tostig was from Wessex; Northumbria was different.	Why was Northumbria different?	Part of Northumbria in Danelaw. Different laws, different language, tax lower.

1.3 The rival claimants for the throne

Source A

Harold, as shown in the Bayeux tapestry.

Harold Godwinson (c1022–1066)

Harold Godwinson was on the spot when King Edward died, as were many of the leading men of the realm. He based his claim on the king's deathbed words, his family connection to him (brother-in-law), his role in recent years as the king's right-hand man, his influence with the earls and thegns, and his proven military prowess. But there were rival claimants to the succession.

Harold Godwinson	
Claim	Appointed as King Edward's successor by the king himself.
Strength of claim	Good – supported by witnesses, but ones loyal to Harold.
Chance of success	Excellent – Harold had the support required to be made king.

Edgar Aethling (c1051–c1126)

There was, in fact, already a natural-born heir to Edward the Confessor. This was Edgar the Aethling. As Edward's nephew, Edgar was directly descended from royal blood, shown by his title 'Aethling', which meant a prince of royal blood. Edward the Confessor and Harold Godwinson had brought Edgar and his father back from Hungary in 1054, where they had gone as exiles after Cnut became king (for more on King Cnut see page 19). Edgar's father promptly died, leaving the six-year-old in Edward's care, although Edward did nothing we know of to boost Edgar's chance of succession. In 1066, the leading men of Anglo-Saxon England, the Witan, knew the threats from Scandinavia and Normandy were very serious and thought a teenage king was not the right choice in such troubled times.

Edgar Aethling	
Claim	Royal blood.
Strength of claim	Strong in theory, but he had no power to back it up.
Chance of success	Weak – although teenagers had become kings before, Anglo-Saxon England at this time needed a warrior-king to defend it against foreign threats.

Harald Hardrada (c1015–1066)

Harald Hardrada was the king of Norway. He was a fearsome old Viking warrior, feared across Europe as well as in other Scandinavian countries. His nickname 'Hardrada' meant 'stern ruler'. His claim to the English throne was based on Viking secret deals and treaties. It is a complicated claim to understand: the key point is that Hardrada believed he had a good enough chance of succeeding to launch an invasion of England.

King Cnut (1016–1035) ruled England as part of a North Sea empire that included Denmark and Norway. When Cnut died, his son, Harthacnut, took the throne. However, shortly afterwards, Harthacnut lost control of Norway to Magnus Olafsson. To avoid war, they agreed a secret treaty that, in the event of one of them dying, the other would be their heir. When Harthacnut died in 1042, Magnus claimed the English throne as well as Harthacnut's Danish one.

Harald Hardrada's constant raiding parties along the Norwegian coast put so much pressure on Magnus that he offered to rule Norway together with Hardrada. This meant that, when Magnus died in 1047, Harald not only gained full control of Norway, he also took on Magnus' claim to England.

It is likely that Hardrada had no major plans to take up his complicated claim to the English throne when Edward the Confessor died. However, this changed when Tostig Godwinson, exiled from England, turned to Hardrada for support. Tostig gave Hardrada the impression that his brother, Harold, was very unpopular in England, especially in the north. Perhaps Tostig also convinced the old Viking that this was his chance for one last glorious adventure.

Harald Hardrada		
Claim	Based on a secret deal about another secret deal made by other Vikings!	
Strength of claim	Weak, although the Danelaw might welcome a Viking king.	
Chance of success	Good, as Harald had perhaps 15,000 warriors and 300 or more Viking longships at his command (together with Tostig's 12 ships), all used to invading the North Sea.	

William of Normandy (c1028–1087)

William was Duke of Normandy, a small country (smaller than Northumbria) surrounded by enemies. He had fought hard to survive since he was very young. England offered the chance of real wealth and power to realise the Normans' ambitious plans throughout Europe.

His claim was based on an agreement William said was made between Edward the Confessor and himself around 1051, an agreement that was then supposedly confirmed by Harold's embassy to Normandy in 1064. William had come to England and Edward had promised him his throne, perhaps if Edward died childless. William managed to obtain the pope's backing for his claim, which proved very important in getting the support William needed for his invasion (see page 34).

William's claim to the English throne was certainly not a surprise to the English in 1066. Harold Godwinson, as King Harold II, started to make preparations to defend England from attack from the south almost immediately after his coronation. In contrast, an attack by Harald Hardrada does not appear to have been anticipated.

Extend your knowledge

Edward and William

Different historians have different interpretations of this agreement. Some deny that any such agreement was possible, others say that Edward was actually a Norman king anyway: he'd grown up in Normandy, modelled Westminster cathedral on Norman cathedrals, and tried to introduce Normans into positions of power when he began his reign in England. Edward certainly needed allies at the time, so it seems logical that he might have made some promises to William.

William of Normandy		
Claim	An agreement with King Edward.	
Strength of claim	Backed by the pope, but lacking evidence.	
Chance of success	Quite good: the Normans were Europe's best warriors, but William would have to find a way to convince his men to risk everything on a very risky invasion attempt and then get his men across the Channel.	

In Anglo-Saxon England, the king could not simply announce his successor: the Witan had a role in selecting the new king. It seems unlikely that the Witan would have accepted William in January 1066: Edward's attempt to bring Normans into senior positions earlier in his reign had been opposed very strongly by all the leading earls, many of whom were still in the Witan.

> ### Activity ?
>
> Divide the class into three groups: Group 1 are Anglo-Saxon actors performing 'The death of Edward the Confessor'; Group 2 is the court of Harald Hardrada; Group 3 is the court of William of Normandy.
>
> a Group 1 needs to plan what their performance is going to show and what they're going to say, before performing it to Groups 2 and 3.
>
> b Groups 2 and 3 need to explain their reactions to the performance to the other groups.

Harold's coronation and reign

Harold Godwinson's coronation (the ceremony where he was crowned king) took place the same day as Edward was buried: 6 January 1066. That was remarkably rapid (Edward had waited for months to be crowned). Everything about the way Harold became king shows him seizing his opportunity.

The Witan

In Anglo-Saxon England, a king's eldest child did not automatically become king when the old king died. Instead, the Witan met to agree who should be king. Often the choice of successor was obvious, but not always. The Witan would be influenced by the needs of the kingdom. Sometimes military strength was more important than being closely related to the dead king.

Because Edward died just after Christmas, and just after the consecration (blessing) of his huge new cathedral in Westminster, a large number of the Witan was already gathered at Edward's palace. Edward died on 5 January and the Witan met on the same day to elect Harold as king. Certainly, the Witan suspected that William would act on his claim to the throne (possibly with Tostig as his ally) and it was probably the need to make preparations for England's defence that made the Witan willing to elect King Harold II as quickly as possible. When news of the coronation reached William, he reacted furiously.

King Harold's challenges

An Anglo-Saxon king only remained in power if he could hold off the challenges of others. Harold faced significant challenges both within England and from outside his realm.

- Challenges from other powerful Anglo-Saxon earls: especially Wessex's old rival, Mercia.
- Acceptance in the north: would Northumbria accept Tostig's brother as king?
- Tostig: Harold's brother was travelling around Europe looking for allies against Harold, as their father, Godwin, had done against King Edward.
- William of Normandy: reports that William was building an invasion fleet soon reached the king.

King Harold's responses

- Straight after his coronation, Harold went to York, the chief city of Northumbria. This was to meet with Witan members who had not been present in London, and to ensure he had their support. It was politically vital that the north did not choose this moment to cause problems.
- He then gathered the largest army England had ever seen. This army was positioned along the south coast of England to defend against invasion. He also stationed a large fleet on the south coast. Both the army and the fleet were levied (raised) from the fyrd.

Tostig gained support in Flanders (he was married to Count Baldwin of Flanders' sister). From Flanders, Tostig sailed a fleet over to England in May 1066. But when he learned about the extraordinary strength of Harold's defences, Tostig left quickly and sailed round the coast to Lincoln, where a fight with the Mercians left Tostig with only 12 ships. He fled Lincolnshire too, for Scotland, and began plotting with Harald Hardrada instead.

Harold's army and fleet guarded the southern coast all summer. Tostig's arrival in May might have triggered these defences earlier than planned. Harold had to keep his army and fleet provisioned: an expensive and complicated business. But the expected Norman invasion did not come. By September, it was time to stand down the army and refit the fleet.

The battles of Gate Fulford and Stamford Bridge

Timeline

Gate Fulford and Stamford Bridge, 1066

8 September Southern fyrd disbanded

20 September The Battle of Gate Fulford; Harold leaves London

19 September Harold hears of Hardrada and Tostig's invasion

25 September The Battle of Stamford Bridge

As summer ended, in September 1066, Harald Hardrada and Tostig launched their attack. Hardrada's fleet numbered around 200–300 warships, carrying perhaps 10,000 Viking. Landing at the River Humber, they marched up to York, which had been the capital of a Viking state only a generation before. Their way was blocked by an army led by Morcar and his elder brother, Edwin, the earls of Northumbria and Mercia, at a place called Gate Fulford. The brothers had decided on open battle to defend York rather than staying behind the security of the city's heavy fortifications.

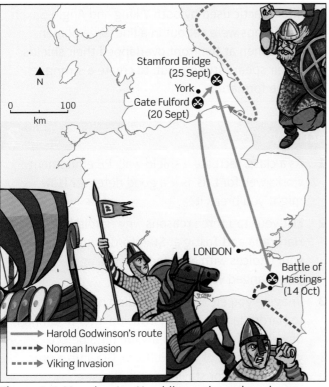

Figure 1.6 Map showing Harold's march north and return south to face invasion of William of Normandy.

Gate Fulford (20 September 1066)

Gate Fulford was a crushing defeat for Edwin and Morcar. There were a number of military reasons for this outcome:

- Edwin and Morcar may have been outnumbered: it is thought they had 6,000 troops against perhaps 9,000 for Hardrada and Tostig (we know some thousands stayed with the ships).
- Hardrada and his housecarls were battle-hardened veterans, and he used a clever strategy in the battle. He positioned Tostig's weaker troops on one wing and, when the English rushed at them, he was able to hit them with his best troops from the side.
- Edwin and Morcar stationed their army with marshland at their backs. This meant their troops had nowhere to go when they were pushed back.

The English army broke and tried to run away into the marsh, but they got stuck in the swampy ground and were cut down. The Norwegians boasted that there were so many dead Englishmen lying in the marsh that they could walk across it without getting their boots muddy.

King Harold's march north

Learning of the invasion (possibly by beacon signals*), Harold took his housecarls north, travelling 185 miles in five days. When he set out, he did not yet know about Gate Fulford.

Key term

Beacon signals*

Fires lit along a chain of high places (cliffs, hill tops) to signal over long distances that an invasion had occurred.

Extend your knowledge

'Marching' north?

The Anglo-Saxon thegns fought on foot, but they travelled to battles on horseback; it is also possible that Harold sailed north, as we know he did take his fleet round the southern coast to London. He would not have taken his southern army with him, however. Harold had already given the order to send the soldiers home – possibly just days before learning of the northern invasion. Harold sent messengers ahead to levy a new army as he travelled, probably most of the troops coming from Essex, East Anglia and some remnants of Edwin and Morcar's troops from Mercia.

Leaving the southern coast was a terrible decision for Harold. However, at the time, Harold must have been confident that it was now too late in the year for William to cross the Channel.

- The first of the September storms had wrecked some of Harold's own fleet and possibly also drove William back from an initial invasion attempt.
- The wind was still blowing from the north when Harold set off, which he knew would prevent William from crossing the Channel.
- Just as Harold had struggled to provide provision for his army, he knew William would have found it difficult to keep his army waiting through the summer.

Harold's five-day forced march north was an outstanding military achievement. It was very difficult to gather thousands of men and bring them all together in such a short time, and what Harold then did with them was a strategic masterstroke.

After the Battle of Gate Fulford, Hardrada and Tostig had exchanged hostages with the city of York, which had surrendered to them without a fight. They had also demanded many more hostages from all over Yorkshire. Hostages assured good faith on both sides of an agreement, as they tended to suffer if an agreement was broken. Hardrada and Tostig were informed that the extra hostages would be handed over to them at a place called Stamford Bridge. On 25 September, they were at Stamford Bridge, awaiting their hostages, when Harold launched a surprise attack.

Stamford Bridge (25 September 1066)

King Harold had probably learned of the hostage deal as he travelled towards York, and decided on his strategy. There was a small hill overlooking Stamford Bridge, which meant that his army could approach undetected. The battle was a complete success for Harold: Hardrada and Tostig were both killed, probably with many thousands of their men. It is reported that only 24 of Hardrada's longships returned, out of the 200 or more that had sailed in August.

Harold's victory was aided by several military factors:

- The Viking army had their weapons and shields with them, but had left their armour on their ships (it was a hot day) as well as perhaps a third of their men.
- Harold succeeded in taking Hardrada and Tostig by surprise; they probably did not know he was even in the area.
- Hardrada's army had fought a battle five days before and were not expecting to fight another.
- The Viking troops felt misled: they had been informed that England hated its new king.
- Harold's housecarls eventually broke the Viking shield wall*. This shows that Harold's men had great endurance as well as formidable battle skills.

Harold had triumphed and secured his kingdom against a very significant threat. However, news soon reached him (on around 1 October) that William of Normandy had landed on the south coast after all, on 28 September. Harold set off south to fight the third and most significant battle of 1066.

Key term

Shield wall*

A military tactic used by both Viking and Anglo-Saxon armies. Troops were set out in a line, several men deep. The men at the front overlapped their shields, with their spears sticking out, to create a strong defensive formation.

Activity

1 As a class, recreate a shield wall. PE equipment works well for this. Is it a good defence? How might you break it?

2 List your top three reasons why Harold beat Hardrada and Tostig at Stamford Bridge. Compare your choices with a partner: do you agree? Have you changed your mind?

3 Imagine you are Harold, deciding how to respond to Hardrada and Tostig's invasion after a summer of waiting for William to invade (and before you've learned of Gate Fulford). Draw up a pros and cons list for staying put in Wessex.

Were the battles significant?

The consequences of both battles were very significant for the following Battle of Hastings. But, there are other factors to consider as well.

Significant because...	However...
Hardrada and Tostig's invasion meant that Harold was not in place to prevent William's invasion.	Harold had already disbanded the southern fyrd in September anyway, as its time was up.
Edwin and Morcar made strategic errors that meant the loss of thousands of men at Gate Fulford (they could have tried staying inside the city walls of York).	Harold was already on his way north before Gate Fulford had been fought. This suggests he didn't think Edwin and Morcar would stop Tostig and Hardrada without his help.
Edwin and Morcar survived Gate Fulford, but it seems they were then unable (or unwilling) to fight with Harold at Hastings. This weakened Harold's army.	This conclusion comes from the fact that Edwin and Morcar aren't mentioned in the sources on the Battle of Hastings: not very strong evidence.
Harold's march south again must have made his remaining housecarls less battle-ready than William's knights.	Harold and his housecarls had just won a victory against the famed Harald Hardrada. Morale must have been high.
Harold's success at taking Hardrada by surprise might have made him over-confident. Instead of waiting for William in fortified London, he rushed to do battle, with fatal consequences.	Harold and the Witan had been waiting and preparing for William for months, perhaps years. A battle on the south coast, on Harold's home turf, may have seemed the best chance of victory.

Activity ?

Concept maps (spider diagrams) are ideal for working out the links between factors and between topics. You can build up a concept map of a topic in three main stages:

a Put your topic (or issue or question) in the middle of a big piece of paper.

b Draw out 'branches' from the central topic to important categories of the topic.

c From those, draw out 'sub-branches' to individual facts or ideas that connect to them.

It is a good idea to colour-code your different categories and add images to make your map memorable.

Try putting together a concept map on 'Harold's problems in 1066'.

Summary

- The rival claimants to the English throne: Edgar Aethling, Harold Godwinson, Harald Hardrada, William of Normandy.
- Harold Godwinson acted quickly to claim the throne, with the Witan's support.
- His preparations for the expected Norman invasion were thorough.
- Harald and Tostig's northern invasion was repulsed, but had serious consequences.

Checkpoint

Strengthen

S1 Describe the claim to the throne of each of the rival claimants.

S2 Give three reasons each that explain the outcomes of the Battles of Gate Fulford and Stamford Bridge.

Challenge

C1 In your own words, summarise the significance of the Battle of Stamford Bridge – why it was important.

C2 How do the events of Harold's coronation relate to how legitimate his claim was to the English throne?

How confident do you feel about your answers to these questions? If you're not sure you have answered them well, try the above study skills activity.

1.4 The Norman invasion

Learning outcomes

- Understand the events and composition of the Battle of Hastings.
- Understand the reasons for William's victory.

Timeline
The Norman invasion, 1066

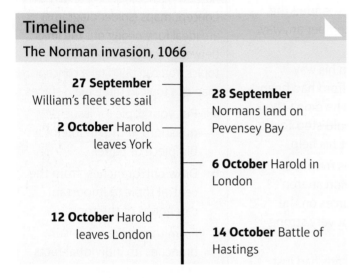

27 September William's fleet sets sail

28 September Normans land on Pevensey Bay

2 October Harold leaves York

6 October Harold in London

12 October Harold leaves London

14 October Battle of Hastings

The Battle of Hastings (14 October 1066)

Although not everything about the Battle of Hastings is clear, some key events are generally agreed.

1. Harold did not achieve surprise

William's scouts informed him about Harold's advance in time for him to leave Hastings and threaten Harold's army as it was gathering together on a wooded hilltop called Caldbec Hill. There was a rush to gain control of the high ground of the battlefield, south of Caldbec Hill, which Harold won, organising his shield wall along a ridge. There was marshland either side of the hill.

2. William sent his foot soldiers in first

The battle lasted eight hours: very long for a medieval battle. William first sent his archers forward, but the English caught the arrows on their shields. Norman foot soldiers then went up the hill towards the shield wall. The heavy axes of the English did a lot of damage. The Norman cavalry then laboured up the hill, but failed to break the wall. The battle started in Harold's favour.

3. William showed his face

Waves of Norman attacks continued throughout the day, with the Anglo-Saxon shield wall standing firm.

At a difficult stage for the Normans, a rumour went round William's army that he had been killed or wounded. William tipped his helmet back to show he was still alive and rallied his troops.

4. Harold's shield wall worn down

A portion of Harold's army disengaged from the shield wall to chase William's men down the hill. They were cut off at the bottom and slaughtered. The Normans gradually reduced the Saxon forces until the shield wall began to break up and became much less effective against cavalry charges.

5. The last stand

Harold, his brothers Gyrth and Leofwine, their housecarls and the remaining fyrd troops held their position at the top of the hill, probably in rings of men around their standards. But they were now heavily outnumbered and unable to hold off the Norman cavalry charges. Harold and his brothers were killed, and their housecarls fought to the last man while the remaining fyrd tried to flee. William was victorious.

Activity ?

Go online and find a site featuring the whole Bayeux Tapestry. Pick one scene from the Battle of Hastings that appeals to you and print it onto A4 paper. Add a caption and labels to the image that include the following information:

a What part of the battle it is showing.

b Who you think the Normans are and who you think the English are (hint: moustaches).

c What you can infer from it about what the battle was like.

The composition of the armies
Elite troops: knights and housecarls

Elite troops are the members of an army that have received special training to fight in a particular way, and are equipped with specialist equipment.

William's knights

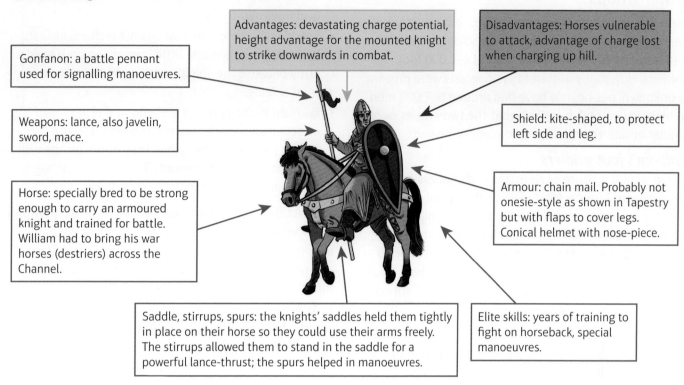

Gonfanon: a battle pennant used for signalling manoeuvres.

Advantages: devastating charge potential, height advantage for the mounted knight to strike downwards in combat.

Disadvantages: Horses vulnerable to attack, advantage of charge lost when charging up hill.

Weapons: lance, also javelin, sword, mace.

Shield: kite-shaped, to protect left side and leg.

Horse: specially bred to be strong enough to carry an armoured knight and trained for battle. William had to bring his war horses (destriers) across the Channel.

Armour: chain mail. Probably not onesie-style as shown in Tapestry but with flaps to cover legs. Conical helmet with nose-piece.

Saddle, stirrups, spurs: the knights' saddles held them tightly in place on their horse so they could use their arms freely. The stirrups allowed them to stand in the saddle for a powerful lance-thrust; the spurs helped in manoeuvres.

Elite skills: years of training to fight on horseback, special manoeuvres.

Figure 1.7 Features of Norman knights.

Harold's housecarls

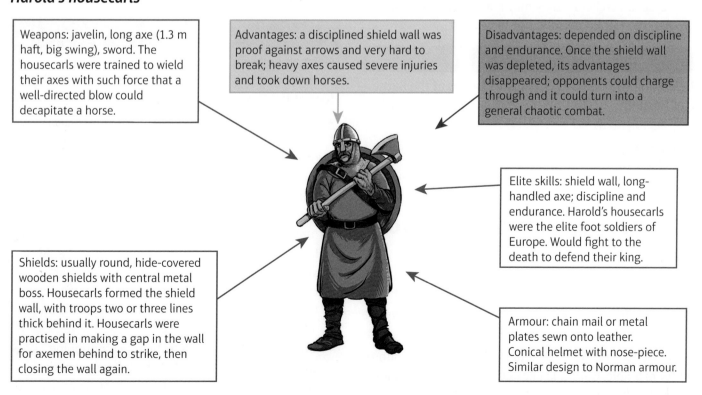

Weapons: javelin, long axe (1.3 m haft, big swing), sword. The housecarls were trained to wield their axes with such force that a well-directed blow could decapitate a horse.

Advantages: a disciplined shield wall was proof against arrows and very hard to break; heavy axes caused severe injuries and took down horses.

Disadvantages: depended on discipline and endurance. Once the shield wall was depleted, its advantages disappeared; opponents could charge through and it could turn into a general chaotic combat.

Shields: usually round, hide-covered wooden shields with central metal boss. Housecarls formed the shield wall, with troops two or three lines thick behind it. Housecarls were practised in making a gap in the wall for axemen behind to strike, then closing the wall again.

Elite skills: shield wall, long-handled axe; discipline and endurance. Harold's housecarls were the elite foot soldiers of Europe. Would fight to the death to defend their king.

Armour: chain mail or metal plates sewn onto leather. Conical helmet with nose-piece. Similar design to Norman armour.

Figure 1.8 Features of Anglo-Saxon housecarls.

Other troops

Both armies had a core of elite troops, but the mass of each army was made up of ordinary soldiers. William had perhaps 800 knights and around 4–6,000 foot soldiers. How many of Harold's housecarls were present is unknown, but he may have had around 6–7,000 men in his army in total. It is likely that the two armies were similar in size, though historians cannot be sure.

William's foot soldiers

These were a mixture of Normans and soldiers-for-hire from all over Europe. Most were probably not trained to fight in co-ordination with the Norman knights. Some of the foot soldiers would have been archers and crossbowmen. Most Norman archers had padded jackets as armour (called gambesons). The others would have been 'heavy' footsoldiers, with chain mail armour, shields and javelins or swords.

Harold's fyrdsmen

Harold's ordinary soldiers were men that he had hastily levied from the fyrd on his trip south. Not all these levies turned up in time and Harold decided to take on William without them. The thegns had good weapons, shields and armour, but the general fyrd may only have had agricultural tools to fight with. There were not many Anglo-Saxon archers – they may have been amongst the troops that Harold decided not to wait for.

Exam-style question, Section B
Describe **two** features of William's troops at the Battle of Hastings.   **4 marks**

Exam tip
Make sure you add supporting information to both.

The reasons for William's victory

Tactics

Because Harold lost the Battle of Hastings, it is tempting to argue that it was because he used old-fashioned tactics against the Norman knights. Is this fair? There are arguments in favour of the shield wall:

- Shield wall tactics were sophisticated. At Gate Fulford, for example, Hardrada allowed the English to attack the weak part of his shield wall, his Flemish troops. As they retreated from the English, he turned his

Viking troops into the flank (side) of the English and overwhelmed them.

- Shield walls were effective against archers. At first, William's archers made little impression on Harold's army because the shield wall caught the arrows on their shields.
- Early on in the battle, the shield wall also proved effective against the Norman cavalry. Because the horses had to charge up hill, they didn't hit the wall fast enough or hard enough. The housecarls' huge battle axes could chop the horses down.

The fact that the battle lasted all day suggests that both sides were evenly matched. However, while the English all fought in the same way, William had a mix of troops and he could use different attacking tactics until he found what worked.

- At first, his archers made little impression on the shield wall: they had to shoot up hill and stay out of the shield wall's javelin range. But, once the wall was depleted, the archers could get closer and be more effective.
- Cavalry were usually only used against enemy cavalry or to chase down fleeing foot soldiers, but William used them against the shield wall. At first, the tactic didn't work but, once the shield wall had been weakened, the mounted knights could charge through and break it up.

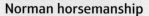

Extend your knowledge

Norman horsemanship

Norman commentators were scornful of the English for not fighting on horseback. However:

- The English had in fact invested instead in a strong fleet. This decision came from their long experience of fighting the Vikings, which was based on the fyrd, fortified towns and a fleet to tackle the Viking longships. If the English fleet had been able to engage the Norman invasion force, this strategy might well have paid off.
- In Normandy, the investment in breeding bigger, stronger horses went alongside long years of training in fighting on horseback. Technological developments were required too: the saddle and stirrups, and also the lance.
- 'Couching' a lance was a technique for gripping the lance in such a way that the full power of the charging horse went into the tip of the lance. This technique was only just getting established in 1066.

Figure 1.8 A plan of the Battle of Hastings, 1066.

Source A

A scene from the Bayeux Tapestry showing the Anglo-Saxon shield wall facing a Norman cavalry charge.

Activity ?

1 Describe two strengths and two weaknesses each of William's troops and Harold's troops.

2 Make two points to support an argument that William's tactics were the reason for his victory at the Battle of Hastings.

3 Anglo-Saxon warriors used horses all the time, but not in battle. What reasons can you think of to explain this?

What weakened the shield wall?

The critical factor in William's victory was therefore the weakening of the shield wall. It is possible that this happened due to a lack of discipline in Harold's army. When Harold's foot soldiers (the general fyrd) broke ranks at the Battle of Hastings, the shield wall began to be badly weakened. It is possible that the English foot soldiers chased retreating Normans because they wanted to grab discarded weapons, armour and horses.

It is also possible that the Norman retreat was a tactic called a 'feigned retreat'. Normans had used this before in battles against the French. A body of troops would pretend to flee in panic, hoping that their opponents would lose their discipline and chase after them. It was very risky, because there was a good chance that a pretend flight could turn into a real one. Medieval battles saw really big casualties only when one side ran away, with the other side chasing them and cutting them down.

Leadership

It is easy to judge Harold for making mistakes in leadership while William made all the right decisions. In fact, both leaders took enormous risks, although they both made these on the basis of decades of military experience. For William, the risks paid off; for Harold, they did not – but it might easily have been the other way around.

William's leadership

Both leaders faced massive organisational challenges: William to prepare his invasion, and Harold to defend against it. Harold's decision to gather his defences early in the summer of 1066 gave William a major opportunity.

- William's long wait through the summer of 1066 was not just because of bad weather for sailing. William knew that, at some point, Harold would have to disband the fyrd and he was waiting for this news. As soon as this happened, William set sail (and hit the same storm that battered Harold's fleet, which William managed to get through). Waiting shows strong strategic leadership from William.

- Keeping his army and fleet together took strong leadership – sources suggest the Norman army gathered at the port of Dives at the start of August. An army takes a lot of feeding and watering – horses as well as men – and William refused to let his soldiers steal food from the surrounding Norman farmers.

- The crossing was also highly ambitious. Transportation of horses in this way had never been done before. The usual process (which the Vikings did, for example) was to find horses in enemy territory as soon as the invaders landed, but the Norman knights could not do this. Their horses were specially bred and trained. Flat-bottomed boats were constructed that horses could be led into. The Bayeux Tapestry depicts this as being a challenging task!

- When William and his troops arrived in Pevensey Bay (a wide bay, ideal for landing from hundreds of ships), he showed strong strategic awareness. The troops marched several miles along the coast to Hastings, where they adapted the Iron Age fort there into a defensible castle. William had organised a 'pre-fabricated' castle to be brought with them from Normandy – prepared in sections that could be put together quickly. This gave his troops some security from attack.

- Once in England, William allowed his men to cause great destruction in the surrounding area. Not only did they take food and drink from the English, and pack horses for transportation, but they laid waste to their surroundings too, burning down houses.

Extend your knowledge

Norman brutality

Some historians think this destruction was a calculated strategy to enrage Harold – this was happening in his home area, after all – to encourage him to come and fight William in open battle. Others would say that the Normans had a reputation throughout Europe for extreme brutality (the 'Harrying of the North' on page 58 is another example) and this was simply their standard way of occupying enemy territory.

Harold's leadership

Harold's military leadership was highly regarded throughout England and it is important not to view the consequences of his decisions out of context. At the time, Harold may have done what he did for very carefully-thought-through reasons. However:

- Calling out his southern army in May was a problem as he then had to maintain it for four months, before finally disbanding it.

Benefits of Harold staying in London	Justifications for Harold's decision
The sources suggest that Harold waited for perhaps five days in London before continuing down to Hastings. He waited there to gather troops. London was well-fortified and William would have had to lay siege to it. This would have been difficult for an invading army to do, as they also needed to find food and infectious diseases (e.g. dysentery) spread very quickly amongst armies in siege conditions.	• If he moved quickly enough, Harold could have bottled William up in Hastings, where he could be starved into submission. Or, Harold might be able to attack William by surprise, as he had done with Hardrada and Tostig.
Criticisms of Harold's decision	• If Harold waited in London, there was a good chance that William would get reinforcements from Normandy.
• In getting down to William as soon as possible, Harold weakened his chances of success because he did not have a full levy of men.	• Anglo-Saxon historians stress that the techniques for defending towns had not developed – Anglo-Saxons were no good at it. William was highly experienced in sieges.
• If he was hoping to surprise William, Harold had underestimated his opponent.	• It is possible that Harold was let down by Edwin and Morcar: perhaps he left without all his troops because the earls of Mercia and Northumbria refused to help him.
• Harold's decision to leave London may have been linked to his outrage at Norman atrocities in Wessex: William may have planned these atrocities so Harold attacked in a rage rather than waiting to be fully prepared.	• Harold was king of England but Wessex was his home. He had a responsibility to protect his countrymen from Norman pillaging.

- Deciding to rush down to fight William in the south was not Harold's only option. He could have waited for William to come to him, in London.
- If Harold had planned on surprising William, in fact it was the other way around. William learned of Harold's muster point from his scouts and arrived there after a long, early morning march from Hastings, before Harold's army were ready.

Leadership and luck

In the chaos of battle, anything could happen. If Harold was hit in the eye by an arrow, as the Bayeux Tapestry possibly shows, then it was a fate that could as easily have happened to William, regardless of all the strengths of his leadership. For example, the Viking sagas recount that Harald Hardrada was killed by an arrow in the throat at Stamford Bridge. For both Normans and Anglo-Saxons, God's will determined the outcome.

Luck (or God's will) did play a significant role in William's victory, which so easily could have gone in Harold's favour. For example:

- Harald Hardarada's invasion to happen when it did: the consequences of the defeat at Gate Fulford and Harold's rapid transit up to York and down again were to weaken Harold's defences.

- William decided to sail for England after winter storms had begun to make the Channel very dangerous. His fleet was very lucky not to have been destroyed.
- Medieval battles were chaotic – the Bayeux Tapestry shows Odo of Bayeux (William's half-brother), for example, having to rally young Norman knights who were panicking. Despite the differences in tactics and troops, the two sides seem to have been evenly matched (this perhaps explains why the battle went on so long). Despite all his planning and tactics, William was also very lucky not to have lost, and perhaps owes his victory to the indiscipline of the fyrd.

Activity ?

There's a thinking skills technique called 'Plus – Minus – Interesting' that is a useful tool for analysis and helps with recalling information, too.

a Plus – write a strength or an advantage of the feature you are studying (e.g. Norman troops).

b Minus – write a weakness or limitation of the feature.

c Interesting – write something you find interesting about the feature.

Try this for the topics in this section: it's especially good for comparing troops, tactics and leadership.

Summary

- The Norman invasion was timed to follow Harold's disbanding of the fyrd.
- An attack late in the year was very risky due to storms in the Channel.
- The Battle of Hastings lasted all day, suggesting the two armies were evenly matched.
- William's victory at the Battle of Hastings has many interlinking causes.

Checkpoint

Strengthen

S1 Describe two features of William's troops.

S2 Describe two features of Harold's troops.

S3 Outline the different stages of the Battle of Hastings.

Challenge

C1 Why do you think Harold lost the Battle of Hastings? Give at least three reasons.

C2 Why do you think William won the Battle of Hastings? Give at least three reasons.

C3 'The English lost because their military tactics and strategies were outdated compared to the Normans.' How far would you agree with this statement?

How confident do you feel about your answers to these questions? If you are not sure you have answered them well, try the above activity.

THINKING HISTORICALLY **Cause and Consequence (3a&b)**

The might of human agency

1 'Our lack of control.' Work in pairs.

Describe to your partner a situation where things did not work out as you had intended. Then explain how you would have done things differently to make the situation as you would have wanted. Your partner will then tell the group about that situation and whether they think that your alternative actions would have had the desired effect.

2 'The tyranny of failed actions.' Work individually.

The first battle of 1066 was Gate Fulford, when the army of Earls Edwin and Morcar attempted to defend the North against invasion by Harald Hardrada.

   a Write down what Morcar's aims were, as Earl of Northumbria.

   b Write down what Morcar's actions were.

   c Write down what the outcome was.

   d In what ways do the outcomes not live up to Morcar's expectations?

   e Now imagine that you are Earl Morcar. Write a defence of your actions. Try to think about the things that you would have known about at the time and make sure that you do not use the benefit of hindsight.

3 'Arguments.' Work in groups of between four and six.

In turn, each group member will read out their defence. Other group members suggest ways to reassure the reader that they were not a failure and that, in some ways, what happened was a good outcome.

4 Think about King Harold and Harald Hardrada's invasion attempt.

   a Write down what you think King Harold's aims were in September 1066. What actions did he take? What were the consequences?

   b In what ways were the consequences of Hardrada's invasion not anticipated by King Harold?

   c In what ways did Hardrada's invasion turn out better for King Harold (in the short-term) than he might have expected?

5 Think about Earl Tostig and Hardrada's invasion attempt of September 1066.

   a In what ways were the consequences of the invasion attempt not anticipated by Tostig?

   b In what ways did Hardrada's invasion attempt turn out worse for Tostig than their intended consequences?

6 To what extent are historical individuals in control of the history they helped to create? Explain your answer with reference to specific historical examples from this topic and others you have studied.

Exam-style question, Section B

Explain why there was a succession crisis after the death of Edward the Confessor.

You may use the following in your answer:

• Normandy   • the Witan.

You **must** also use information of your own.   **12 marks**

Exam tip

This question is about causation. Six marks are for knowledge and understanding, six are for your analysis skills, so do not just describe what happened after January 1066. You need to identify the features of the succession crisis, then develop evidence to support each point.

Recap: Anglo-Saxon England and the Norman Conquest, 1060–66

Recall quiz

1 Who was the king of England before Harold?
2 Where was Harald Hardrada king of?
3 Name three of Harold Godwinson's brothers.
4 What was a burh?
5 What was the name for a 'free farmer' in Anglo-Saxon England?
6 List the four main claimants to the English throne after Edward died in January 1066.
7 Who won at Gate Fulford?
8 Who won at Stamford Bridge?
9 Name a tactic used by William at the Battle of Hastings.
10 Two of Harold's brothers died with him at the Battle of Hastings. What were their names and where were they earls of?

Source A

An Anglo-Saxon poem about a great English battle against the Vikings, which ended in an English defeat (the Battle of Maldon, 991), has a thegn saying:

I give you my word that I will not retreat
One inch; I shall forge on
And avenge my lord in battle.
Now that he has fallen in the fight
No loyal warrior living [...]
Need reproach me for returning home lordless
In unworthy retreat, for the weapon shall take me,
The iron sword.

Exam-style question, Section B

'The main reason for the English defeat at the Battle of Hastings was superior Norman tactics.'

How far do you agree? Explain your answer.

You may use the following in your answer:

• the feigned retreat
• the shield wall.

You **must** also use information of your own. **16 marks**

Exam tip

This is a question about cause. Remember that 'How far do you agree?' always means the need for analysis of points that support the statement and points that support other causes. The information provided to help you can be used in your answer, but remember that not adding an extra point of your own limits the number of marks.

Activities

1 Anglo-Saxons wrote epic poetry about bravery in battle and the honour of dying for their lord. Write a poem of your own, expressing the feelings of an Anglo-Saxon thegn who fought with Harold at the Battle of Hastings. Make it as epic as possible.

2 Put together a news-style report on the contenders for the throne of England following Edward's death in January 1066. Role-play interviews with the main contenders (make sure you use appropriate accents – you'll need a Hungarian accent for Edgar).

3 Draw a big concept map (spider diagram) for the topic: Reasons for William's victory. You will need to decide on some categories for your diagram – for example, tactics, luck, leadership, troops. Use A3 paper and colour-code your categories to help make them more memorable.

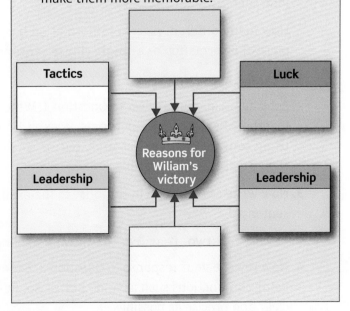

Writing historically: managing sentences

Successful historical writing is clearly expressed, using carefully managed sentence structures.

Learning outcomes

By the end of this lesson, you will understand how to:

- select and use single clause and multiple clause sentences.

Definitions

Clause: a group of words or unit of meaning that contains a verb and can form part or all of a sentence, e.g. 'William I conquered the Anglo-Saxons'.

Single clause sentence: a sentence containing just one clause, e.g. 'William I conquered the Anglo-Saxons.'

Multiple clause sentence: a sentence containing two or more clauses, often linked with a conjunction, e.g. 'William I conquered the Anglo-Saxons and ruled England for 21 years'.

Co-ordinating conjunction: a word used to link two clauses of equal importance within a sentence, e.g. 'and', 'but', 'so', 'or', etc.

How can I structure my sentences clearly?

When you are explaining and exploring complex events and ideas, you can end up writing very long sentences. These can make your writing difficult for the reader to follow.

Look at the extract below from a response to this exam-style question:

> Describe **two** features of the social system of Anglo-Saxon England. **(4 marks)**

> *Someone's position in Anglo-Saxon society depended on how much land they owned but the thegns who were the local lords could lose their land and become peasants or slaves and the ceorls who were free farmers could rise to become thegns.*

1. The writer of the response above has linked every piece of information in his answer into one, very long sentence.

   How many different pieces of information has the writer included in this answer? Re-write each piece of information as a **single clause sentence**. For example:

> *The thegns were local lords.*

2. Look again at your answer to Question 1. Which of the single clause sentences would you link together? Rewrite the response twice, experimenting with linking different sentences together using **conjunctions** such as 'and', 'but' or 'so'. Remember: you are aiming to make your writing as clear and precise as possible.

3. Now write a paragraph in response to the exam-style question below, using only single clause sentences.

> Describe **two** features of towns in Anglo-Saxon England. **(4 marks)**

4. Now rewrite your response to Question 3. Experiment with linking different sentences together using conjunctions such as 'and', 'but' or 'so'. Remember: you are aiming to make your writing as clear and precise as possible.

How can I use conjunctions to link my ideas?

There are several types of **multiple clause sentence** structures that you can use to link your ideas.

If you want to balance or contrast two ideas of equal importance within a sentence, you can use co-ordinating conjunctions to link them.

Look at the extract below from a response to this exam-style question:

> Explain why William won the Battle of Hastings. **(12 marks)**

> *William's leadership was a key reason for his success. He waited for Harold to disband the fyrd and kept his forces together and sailed as soon as he heard. This not only weakened Harold's forces but also took Harold by surprise. In the end he won not through tactics but because the Saxons were unprepared and rushing from fighting the Vikings.*

These co-ordinating conjunctions link equally important actions that happened at the same time.

These paired co-ordinating conjunctions contrast two possible causes.

These paired co-ordinating conjunctions link and balance two equally important ideas.

5. How else could the writer of the response above have linked, balanced or contrasted these ideas? Experiment with rewriting the response, using different sentence structures and different ways of linking ideas within them.

Did you notice?

The first sentence in the response above is a single clause sentence:

> *William's leadership was a key reason for his success.*

6. Why do you think the writer chose to give this point additional emphasis by structuring it as a short, single clause sentence? Write a sentence or two explaining your ideas.

Improving an answer

Now look at the final paragraph below, which shows a response to the exam-style question above.

> *William's patience and leadership gave him an advantage. William's preparations were thorough. Harold's position was growing weaker. Many of the Anglo-Saxon warriors had fought and marched already. The Anglo-Saxons were exhausted. William's tactics were clever. His varied tactics took advantage of the luck he had.*

Rewrite this paragraph, choosing some conjunctions from the **Co-ordinating Conjunction Bank** below to link, balance or contrast the writer's ideas.

Co-ordinating Conjunction Bank	
and	not only… but also…
but	either… or…
or	neither… nor…
so	both… and…

02 | William I in power: securing the kingdom, 1066–87

William had won the Battle of Hastings in 1066, and destroyed the power of King Harold and the Godwinsons. However, it would take many more years of fighting before William could feel secure as king of England. Although the leaders of Anglo-Saxon society, the earls, Church leaders and their thegns, chose to accept William as king in 1066 rather than fight another battle against him, resistance to Norman rule grew. William needed to reward his followers with land and money, which meant Anglo-Saxons losing land to Normans, and Anglo-Saxons paying money for Normandy's benefit.

People resist rulers in lots of different ways – from making jokes about them behind their backs to assassinating them. Rebellion is when people rise up against their rulers and fight them. If the rebellion is successful, the leaders will be replaced. If a rebellion fails, the consequences for the rebels are usually fatal. The Normans were able to defeat the Anglo-Saxon rebellions of 1068–71 and impose control over the rebellious areas. Key to this control were castles – for most of England, castles were something completely new.

From their castles, the Norman conquerors were able to impose other methods of control, too. The most significant long-term method was a social and economic one – the Normans took away Anglo-Saxon control of the land. By 1075, the kingdom was secure from Anglo-Saxon rebellions. Unfortunately for William, however, he then faced a revolt from his own men when some of his own followers turned against him and challenged his control over the kingdom.

Learning outcomes

In this chapter you will find out:

- the ways in which the Normans started to gain control of England after 1066

- why there was Anglo-Saxon resistance to the Normans and what form it took

- the consequences of Anglo-Saxon resistance on the way William ruled England

- why some of William's own men revolted against him in 1075 and what the effects were of this 'Revolt of the Earls'.

The submission of the earls, 1066

What happened after the Battle of Hastings?

William and his surviving troops returned to Hastings after the battle. He waited there to see if the Anglo-Saxon nobles would come and surrender to him, accepting that his victory at Hastings now made William king of England. No one came.

Survivors from Harold's army fled back to London, where they met up with the troops who had arrived there after Harold had marched south. The Witan elected Edgar Aethling as king. Stigand, Archbishop of Canterbury and Ealdred, Archbishop of York were involved in making Edgar king, and Earls Edwin and Morcar also supported Edgar. It is not clear if Edwin and Morcar fought at Hastings or not, but we do know they were in London after the battle, and that they sent their sister, Ealdgyth, Harold's widow, to Chester where it was safer. This suggests that London was preparing for a fight.

It was important for William to get the south coast of England under his control so that reinforcements and supplies could be brought over from Normandy. He also sent troops to seize Winchester, where England's royal treasury was held. However, when he and his troops reached Dover, many became very ill, including William. If the Anglo-Saxons had attacked at this point, it is likely that William would have been defeated.

The march on London

Once his supply route from Normandy to England was secure, William led his troops on a march from the south coast to London. If the Anglo-Saxons were not going to come to him to surrender, it was clear that he would have to go to them and force their submission. As they went, the Normans destroyed homes and farms – as William had done around Hastings at the start of the invasion. Intimidated, the inhabitants of towns on the way to London surrendered to William as fast as they could. However, London was a fortified city, with strong stone walls, and did not surrender. Instead of attacking it directly, William led his troops west, continuing their path of destruction, until they reached Berkhamstead.

The submission* at Berkhamstead

When William reached Berkhamstead, he was met by Edgar Aethling, together with leading men of London, Archbishop Ealdred and both Edwin and Morcar. They submitted to William, swore oaths to obey him and gave him hostages to guarantee their promises. They offered him the crown. In return, William promised to be a 'gracious lord' to them.

Key term

Submission*
Formal acceptance of and surrender to authority.

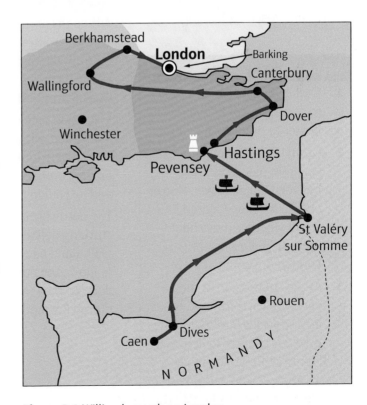

Figure 2.1 William's march on London.

Extend your knowledge

William's march

Since Archbishop Stigand had already met William at Wallingford, it seems likely that he negotiated the surrender in advance. Wallingford is about 30 km west of London.

Sources also claim Edwin and Morcar submitted to William at Barking, 10 km east of London: so perhaps they were forced to submit twice.

Using an online map like Google Maps™, plot a more detailed map of William's route using Figure 2.1 as a starting point. How would you describe the route William took?

It is thought that William and many of his men were ill for a month in Dover. William's march is about 300 km and his army probably marched 30 km per day. Estimate dates for the start of the march and reaching Barking.

Activities ?

1. Explain Edgar Aethling's claim to the throne of England in a poster to promote his cause.

2. Using the table to help you, role-play a discussion between Edgar, Edwin, Morcar and Archbishop Ealdred about whether they should fight, sit out a siege of London or submit.

3. At the submission of the earls, William promised to be a 'gracious lord'. Using the previous chapter to help you, identify three things that an Anglo-Saxon earl would expect a 'gracious lord' to do.

Why did the earls submit in 1066?

It is not clear why the Anglo-Saxon earls submitted to the Normans in 1066, as on balance, their position seemed stronger than the Normans' position.

However, the earls clearly felt that submission was better than fighting, and it is true that their position had significant weaknesses, while the Normans had some key strengths.

Strengths of the earls' position	Weaknesses of William's position 
London was strongly **fortified** and William would lose a lot of men if he attacked it directly.	William and his troops were deep into enemy territory with no secure place to retreat to.
The earls and other leading noblemen had rallied around Edgar, who had a much better claim to the throne than William.	William's claim to the throne was irrelevant if the **Witan** had already chosen a new king, backed by the Church.
William might have gained control of the earldom of Wessex, but Mercia (Edwin) and Northumbria (Morcar) were the two next strongest earldoms, representing over half the country.	William's troops may have been **reinforced** from Normandy, but the numbers in his army were tiny (possibly 5,000) compared to a fyrd levied from the earls. Many Normans had also recently been very ill.
Weaknesses of the earls' position	**Strengths of William's position**
Although London was a stronghold, William's route threatened to cut it off from reinforcements from the north. He may also have spotted weaknesses in the defences.	William acted quickly to seize Winchester. That gave him control of the **royal treasury**. Without his treasury, Edgar could not reward followers, while William could.
Edgar had only recently arrived in England, without ready-made support. He took no decisive action as king, probably because the earls and he couldn't agree on what to do.	Although his army was weakened by battle and illness, William was an extremely **effective** leader. His followers continued to obey him despite all the dangers.
The Battle of Hastings had been a crushing defeat. The best warriors in England had been killed. Many Anglo-Saxons thought that God had decided they should lose in order to punish England for being sinful.	Destroying everything in the path of his army with fire and the sword was a **brutally effective** strategy for William that did not require huge troop numbers. People rushed to submit to William rather than face destruction.

Rewarding followers and establishing control on the borderlands

On 25 December 1066, William was crowned king of England by Archbishop Ealdred in Westminster cathedral, the burial place of Edward the Confessor. At his coronation, William swore an oath that he would rule England like the best Anglo-Saxon kings had, if the English people would be loyal to him.

Source A

This extract from the Anglo-Saxon Chronicle's entry for 1066 describes William's coronation. This version of the Chronicle was written in Worcester.

[A]nd William gave a pledge on the Gospels, and swore an oath besides, before [Archbishop] Ealdred would place the crown on his head, that he would govern this nation according to the best practice of his predecessors if they would be loyal to him. Nevertheless he imposed a very heavy tax on the country, and went oversea to Normandy in the spring.

Rewarding Anglo-Saxon loyalty

The Anglo-Saxon aristocracy would have understood this oath to mean that William was going to be a king like Edward the Confessor. Historians agree that William also wanted a trouble-free takeover, with Anglo-Saxons continuing to have important roles in government. Earls like Edwin and Morcar kept their earldoms, archbishops like Stigand and Ealdred kept their positions. A Northumbrian lord, Gospatric, was made Earl of northern Northumbria after paying William a large amount of money. William also offered rewards for Anglo-Saxon loyalty. He promised that Edwin could marry his daughter, which would have made Edwin very powerful in the new kingdom if it had happened.

Rewarding William's followers

A problem with the plan for a trouble-free takeover, however, was that William also needed to reward his own followers. He had convinced people to join his invasion with the promise of land, and he had hired mercenaries from all along the coast of north-west Europe with the promise of money.

William went about making good on his promises in three ways:

- He sent **rich gifts** to the pope and to Church supporters in Normandy, probably from the royal treasury at Winchester.
- Soon after his coronation, he set a **geld tax**. We do not know how much, but it was described as being 'very heavy' (see Source A). This would have brought in revenue to pay his mercenaries.
- He declared that, as king, all the **land** in England now belonged to him. He was free to grant this land to those who had served him well.

William said that all those who had fought against him at Hastings had lost the right to their lands. This gave him all the lands of the Godwinsons, for example, including Wessex, the richest earldom of all. As king, Harold had also inherited all the royal estates from Edward. William kept much of this land for himself (around a fifth of all the land in England was crown land), but that still left a huge amount to grant to his followers.

The biggest winners of William's followers were his family and closest advisers, almost all of whom were Normans and none of whom were Anglo-Saxons. While the Anglo-Saxon aristocracy might have hoped for some of Harold's lands, it was accepted in Anglo-Saxon society that a victorious king would reward his own followers with the lands and treasure of his defeated foe. Previous Anglo-Saxon and Danish kings had done the same.

Extend your knowledge

Rewarding loyalty

William used the Godwinsons' earldoms to reward three key followers in particular:

- William's half-brother, Odo, Bishop of Bayeux, received all of Kent (William made him Earl of Kent at Dover, before the earls had even submitted).
- William FitzOsbern, one of William's most trusted advisers (and a relative), was granted the Isle of Wight, much of Hampshire and large areas in the west.
- Robert of Montgomery, who had governed Normandy in William's absence, was rewarded with land in Essex and Sussex, and made Earl of Shrewsbury.

Establishing control on the borderlands

Wales had been a threat to Edward the Confessor's rule and William wanted the border between England and Wales to be made secure. Previous Anglo-Saxon kings had built their own defences along the borderland with Wales (called the March* of Wales).

William established three new earldoms centred on Hereford, Shrewsbury and Chester. These were called the Marcher earldoms.

> **Key term**
>
> **March***
>
> An Anglo-Saxon term for border.

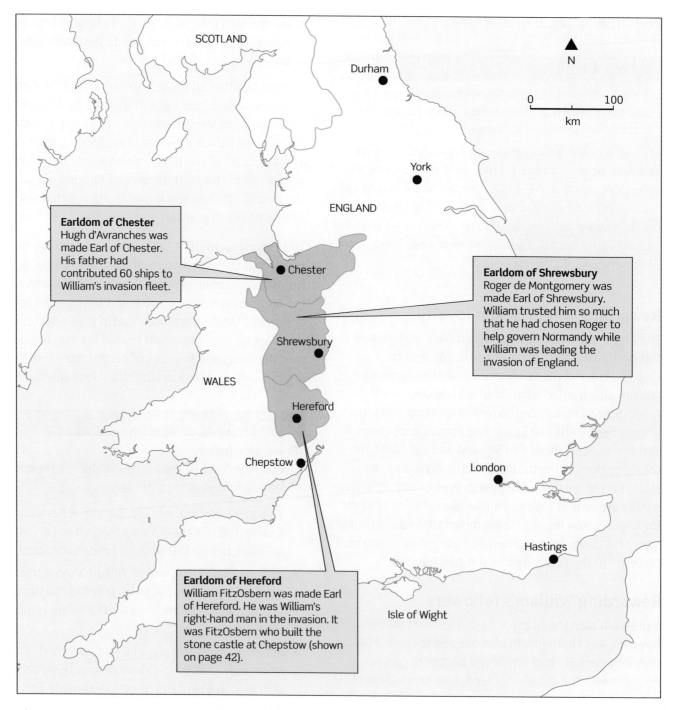

Earldom of Chester
Hugh d'Avranches was made Earl of Chester. His father had contributed 60 ships to William's invasion fleet.

Earldom of Shrewsbury
Roger de Montgomery was made Earl of Shrewsbury. William trusted him so much that he had chosen Roger to help govern Normandy while William was leading the invasion of England.

Earldom of Hereford
William FitzOsbern was made Earl of Hereford. He was William's right-hand man in the invasion. It was FitzOsbern who built the stone castle at Chepstow (shown on page 42).

Figure 2.2 The Marcher earldoms of Chester, Shrewsbury and Hereford protected England from Wales.

Key features of the Marcher earldoms

Key feature	Details	Purpose
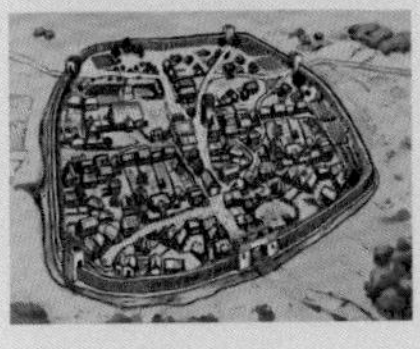 Shire-sized, centred on shire town	While the great earldoms of Anglo-Saxon England were big areas containing several shires, the Marcher earldoms were smaller and more compact.	Their size made them easier to control, but also ensured the Marcher earls were not as powerful as the king.
 Special privileges to create settlements	The Marcher earldoms gave their earls the rights that usually only the king had: to create boroughs (towns) and markets, and to establish churches (replacing Anglo-Saxon ones).	These rights helped the earls to attract people from Normandy to come and settle the frontier regions: colonisation*.
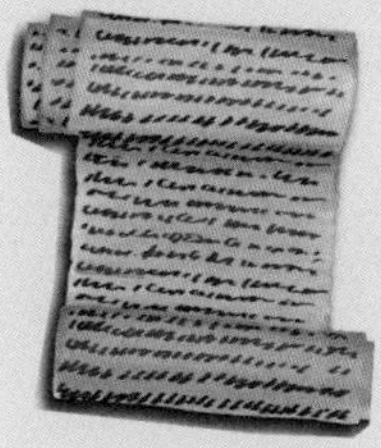 Granted the full power of the law	Usually, sheriffs were the king's officers, but in the Marcher earldoms, sheriffs worked for the earl. Sheriffs controlled the shire courts and this gave the earls almost complete power over the legal system in the earldom.	The earls became the central figures of law and could respond quickly and firmly to any unrest or disobedience.
 Exempted from tax	Earls did not have to pay tax to the king on their lands in Marcher earldoms, unlike earls in the rest of England.	To reward their loyalty and encourage the earls to spend out on new settlements and defences.
 The right to build castles	In the rest of England, landholders had to apply to the king before they could build castles; the Marcher earls were free to build them wherever they were needed.	Castles were used to control the area and to launch attacks into Wales. They were essential to controlling the Marches.

Key term

Colonisation*

When one country encourages the migration of its people to another country.

The men who controlled this frontier, the Marcher earls, therefore had a lot more independence from the king than other earls and that enabled them to deal with trouble directly and rapidly. However, they were not the king's equals. They gave their allegiance to the king and had to provide military service for him whenever he required it. They were not allowed to try people for crimes against the king either.

Exam-style question, Section B

Explain why William created the Marcher earldoms.

You may use the following in your answer:

* protecting the borders
* rewarding followers.

You **must** also use information of your own. **12 marks**

Exam tip

This question is about causation. Some things in history happened because people intended them to happen. Here you can explain what William wanted to achieve as a result of the creation of the Marcher earldoms. Write an explanation, not a description.

Reasons for building castles

Castles were key to the way William established control over England. It is estimated that 500 were built during his reign. Although castles were common in Normandy and north-west Europe, they were almost unknown in Anglo-Saxon England and very different from the fortified burhs of the shires. One of the first things that William did when he invaded was to build a castle at Pevensey, where he landed.

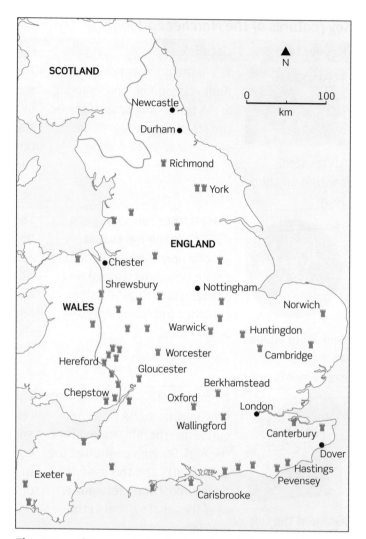

Figure 2.3 This map shows the location of the most important castles built during William's reign.

Key features and advantages of castles

The design of motte* and bailey* castles made them quick to build and difficult to attack.

Activities

1   Explain, using the map in Figure 2.3 to help you, why castles are clustered together in some locations. What is significant about those locations? Discuss with your partner.

2   Use Figure 2.4 on the opposite page to help you:

   a   plan how you would attack the castle

   b   plan how you would defend it.

Key terms

Motte*

The mound of earth that the castle stood on.

Bailey*

The outer part of the castle, surrounding the motte and protected by a fence or wall.

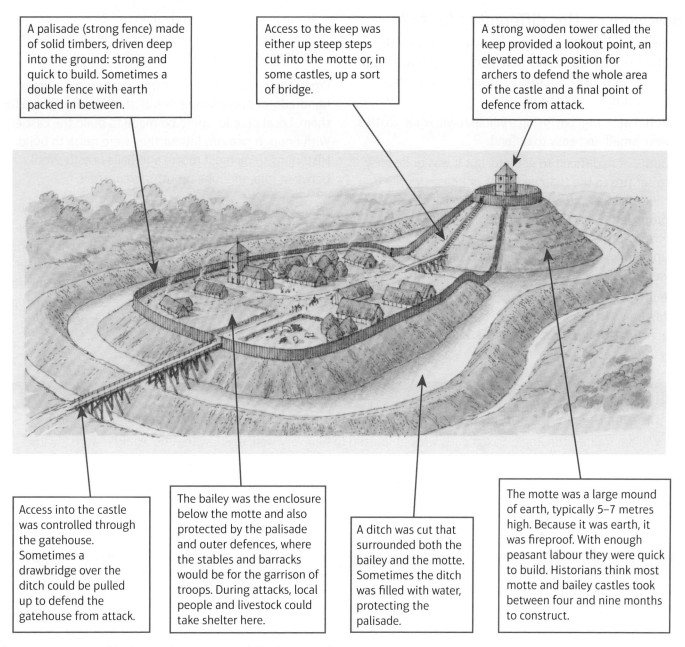

A palisade (strong fence) made of solid timbers, driven deep into the ground: strong and quick to build. Sometimes a double fence with earth packed in between.

Access to the keep was either up steep steps cut into the motte or, in some castles, up a sort of bridge.

A strong wooden tower called the keep provided a lookout point, an elevated attack position for archers to defend the whole area of the castle and a final point of defence from attack.

Access into the castle was controlled through the gatehouse. Sometimes a drawbridge over the ditch could be pulled up to defend the gatehouse from attack.

The bailey was the enclosure below the motte and also protected by the palisade and outer defences, where the stables and barracks would be for the garrison of troops. During attacks, local people and livestock could take shelter here.

A ditch was cut that surrounded both the bailey and the motte. Sometimes the ditch was filled with water, protecting the palisade.

The motte was a large mound of earth, typically 5–7 metres high. Because it was earth, it was fireproof. With enough peasant labour they were quick to build. Historians think most motte and bailey castles took between four and nine months to construct.

Figure 2.4 Motte and bailey castles were very difficult to attack.

Why were castles important?

- They were built in **strategic locations** – for example, at river crossings or near passes through mountains or hills. The Marcher earls built castles all along the border with Wales, as shown in Figure 2.3.

- They were used as a **base** by the lord of the area. The Marcher earls, for example, launched invasions into Wales from castles like Chepstow in South Wales. If troops were beaten back, they could take refuge in the castle and then launch a counter-attack.

- They were used to **dominate territory** newly brought under Norman control. These castles were often built in towns. Exeter, Warwick, Nottingham and York castles were all built as part of campaigns against unrest in the area.

- They were a **symbol of Norman power**: everyone in the area would see the castle towering over them and would constantly be reminded of who ruled them.

How were castles different to burhs?

- Burhs were **public**, maintained by the town for the protection of all; castles were generally **private**, built for the lord and his garrison (troops who defended the castle).

- Burhs were **big**, enclosing a whole town, while castles were **small** and easy to defend.

- Burhs were difficult to get into, but it was quite easy to set **fire** to the thatched roofs of houses within them. Castles, although made of wood, were also protected by earthworks. Additionally, they were not easy to set on fire because the motte raised the keep up high and it could also be **protected** from fire with wetted animal skins.

- Burhs had been designed to **protect** Anglo-Saxons; castles were used to **control** them. In rebellious areas, castles were spaced at 32 km intervals.

Norman troops could travel up to 32 km in a day, meaning that unrest anywhere in the area could be dealt with very quickly.

When castles were built in towns, dozens, sometimes hundreds, of houses were demolished to make room for them. Local people would be made to build the castle. With enough peasant labour they were quick to build. Historians think most motte and bailey castles took between four and nine months to constuct.

Troops would be based in the castle's garrison, ready to crack down on any troublemakers. The local skyline would be dominated by the castle, a constant reminder of who was now in charge. The Anglo-Saxon Chronicle for 1067 says the Normans in that year 'built castles far and wide throughout the land, oppressing the unhappy people, and things went ever from bad to worse'.

Summary

- The submission of the earls in 1066 suggested that William could be accepted as king.
- William treated the Anglo-Saxon earls who submitted to him very well, to show that he would reward loyalty.
- However, he needed to reward his followers and supporters, too, with land and money.
- William set up new earldoms to help establish control over the English borderlands.
- Castles, new to England, were very important in establishing military control.

Checkpoint

Strengthen

S1 Give three reasons that help explain the submission of the earls.

S2 Give one example of how William rewarded a Norman follower and one example of how he rewarded a loyal Anglo-Saxon.

S3 Describe three features of Norman castles that made them effective against unrest.

Challenge

C1 Explain how the Marcher earldoms were different from Anglo-Saxon earldoms.

C2 Outline the strengths and weaknesses of William's position by Christmas 1066.

How confident do you feel about your answers to these questions? If you are not sure you answered them well, try the following activity.

Activity

The '5Ws' technique is an excellent way of generating ideas, aiding recall and identifying gaps in your knowledge. Ask yourself: Who, what, when, where and why? Try it for castles.

The revolt of Edwin and Morcar in 1068

Soon after the coronation, in spring 1067, William felt England was secure enough for him to return home to Normandy in triumph. He took with him Edgar Aethling, Earl Edwin, Earl Morcar, Earl Waltheof and many other Anglo-Saxon aristocrats, plus a lot of English treasure.

By the time William returned to England in December 1067, Norman control was under threat. For example, Herefordshire had been attacked by the Welsh and a rebel Anglo-Saxon thegn, Eadric the Wild.

Events of the revolt

In 1068, Edwin and Morcar fled from William's court. They went north and were joined by many others in rebellion against William, all protesting at the injustice and tyranny of his rule. We do not know a great deal about the other supporters of this revolt: Bleddyn, Lord of Powys (in Wales) was one, also Maerleswein, the sheriff of Yorkshire, Earls Waltheof and Gospatric of Northumbria – and Edgar Aethling.

Key term

Castellan*

The governor of a castle and its surrounding lands (castlery); its lord or a steward of the local lord.

Figure 2.5 The causes of the revolt.

Edwin's resentment
William promised Edwin could marry his daughter, but then went back on his word. William allowed Edwin to keep his earldom, but made it much smaller and less important.

Bad government
Odo of Bayeux and William FitzOsbern were reported to have seized land from Anglo-Saxons unlawfully and allowed their soldiers to rape Anglo-Saxon women without punishment during their vice regency.

Morcar's resentment
Morcar's earldom was also reduced in size. William granted the northern part of Northumbria to Tostig's old thegn, Copsi, who had shown proper submission to William. Maerleswein, a former steward of King Harold, was granted control over parts of Yorkshire. Loss of land meant a loss of power and money.

Causes of the revolt

The loss of lands
The Anglo-Saxon Chronicle for 1067 reports: 'When William returned (from Normandy in 1067) he gave away every man's land'. Odo and FitzOsbern's land grabs were repeated all over the country, with William's followers seeking to expand their grants by every means possible.

Castles
Castles were resented wherever they appeared as they were the symbol of Norman domination and the centre of Norman control over an area.
Castleries were set up: units of land controlled by the castellan* of a castle, who could call on the people in that area to provide things the castle and its garrison required. Castle-building in towns also meant the clearance of dozens, sometimes hundreds, of homes.

Taxes
William's heavy geld tax of December 1066 was resented. It is likely that the Anglo-Saxon earls who were taken back to Normandy recognised that William planned to use English wealth for the good of Normandy, which would not benefit them.

When William was informed of the revolt, he took his forces north, building castles as they went. William went first to Warwick, a key city in Mercia, set about building a castle and then went to Nottingham and built another. It was a very successful show of force. Edwin and Morcar were quick to surrender as soon as William had established control of Warwick. The citizens of York sent William hostages to show their obedience as soon as Nottingham had fallen, followed quickly by the Northumbrian rebels. Edgar fled north to Scotland, where Malcolm III took him in; the others begged William for forgiveness. The revolt was over, but resistance continued.

Threats on the borderlands

The Marcher earls led raids and full-scale invasions into Wales, which were clearly a threat to the Welsh kings. Rebellions against William in England could count on Welsh support.

Outcomes of the revolt and reasons for its failure

- The revolt collapsed very quickly after Edwin and Morcar surrendered. William pardoned them, but kept them as 'guests' at his court, where he could keep them under control. They escaped (again) in 1071 (see page 55), when it seemed likely that William was about to imprison them.

- The escape of Edgar Aethling and the other rebel leaders to Scotland created a new centre of resistance to William's control. This was important for the next big rebellion against William in 1069.

- Although Edwin and Morcar's revolt had gathered support from all over the country, William's awesome show of strength would have convinced many that further revolt was useless.

- Why did Edwin and Morcar surrender so quickly? One reason could be that their revolt of 1068 was a test to see whether William was able to respond. As soon as Mercian and Northumbrian cities submitted to William's authority, the rebels decided to wait for a better opportunity.

- It is also likely that the rebels were not united by a common cause, but each had their own resentments. Perhaps Edwin and Morcar hoped that William would return all their lands to them if they threatened his control over Mercia and Northumbria.

- One reason why William had no need to compromise with the rebels was that his castle-building proved exceptionally effective at imposing control (see Source A).

Source A

An Anglo-Norman English chronicler, Orderic Vitalis, writing soon after the revolt.

The fortifications that the Normans called castles were scarcely known in the English provinces, and so the English – in spite of their courage and love of fighting – could put up only a weak resistance to their enemies.

Activities ?

1. Create a poster that calls on your fellow Anglo-Saxons to join the rebellion against William and the Norman oppressors. Use the information about the causes of the revolt to help you.

2. Which of the following categories would you find useful in identifying the different types of reason that contributed to the revolt of 1068: social, political, economic, military and religious? Find ways to link them: for example, grievances over loss of land combined loss of power and loss of money.

3. Compare Edwin and Morcar's revolt with Tostig's revolt against Edward and Harold. What are the similarities and what are the differences? Consider both features of the rebellions and motives for the rebellions.

Edgar the Aethling and the rebellions in the North, 1069

In the spring of 1069, a series of rebellions began in the North that were extremely dangerous for William because of the combination of forces involved:

- Rebels from Northumbria joined forces with Edgar the Aethling.
- Edgar had the backing of Malcolm III (Edgar's sister had married Malcolm).
- King Sweyn of Denmark sent a fleet of ships and warriors led by his brother, Asbjorn. This enormous force teamed up with Edgar and the other rebels.

The death of Robert Cumin

After being betrayed by Gospatric in the revolt of Edwin and Morcar, William chose a new Earl of northern Northumbria: Robert Cumin, one of his supporters. In January 1069, Cumin took a large force north, launching attacks on towns and villages on his way. When he got to Durham, the bishop there warned him that this violence had caused great resentment, but his troops carried on looting regardless. This was a serious mistake. They were taken by surprise by a band of Northumbrians, who slaughtered them in the streets of Durham. Cumin took refuge in the bishop's house, but the rebels set fire to it and killed him when he was forced out by the flames.

The uprising in York

Soon after Cumin's murder, a similar uprising occurred in York, which killed the governor and many Norman troops. Edgar the Aethling and his supporters came down from Scotland and joined the rebels, launching an attack on the Norman sheriff and his garrison. It's possible that the Normans were able to hold out in York castle until a message reached William, who arrived very quickly and with a large army. William routed the rebels, with the whole city of York being laid to waste. Edgar escaped back to Scotland. A new castle was rapidly built, with William FitzOsbern as its castellan. The king decided that FitzOsbern would be able to keep the North under control while he returned to Winchester to celebrate Easter. This shows how important it was for William to be seen acting out the ceremonies of being king, but he had underestimated the threat to his rule. The Northern rebellions were far from over.

Timeline

The rebellions in the North, 1069

31 January Earl Cumin is killed in Durham

c.February Uprising in York. Edgar joins uprising from Scotland. William defeats York rebels

13 April William back in Winchester for Easter

c.8 September Danish fleet invades on the east coast

21 September Combined Anglo–Danish army arrives at York

c.December William pays the Danes to go away

Events of the rebellions

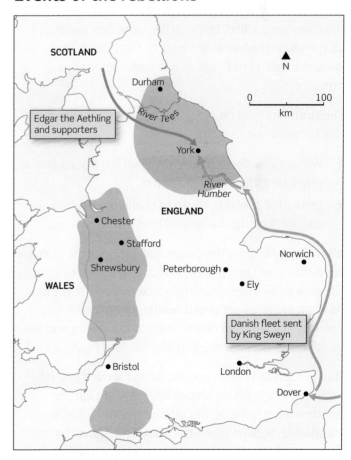

Figure 2.6 The rebellions started in the North, but also included Shropshire in the west, Devon in the south-west and Staffordshire in the north midlands.

The Anglo–Danish attack on York

Through the summer of 1069, King Sweyn of Denmark assembled a fleet, which arrived on the English coast at the start of September. Large invasion fleets were only put together if the chances of success seemed good enough to unite all the different Viking warlords involved. It is likely, therefore, that the Danes believed William was vulnerable.

Raiding up the east coast, the Danes met up with Edgar's troops (down again from Scotland) in mid-September. This co-ordinated attack was a significant threat to William. Not only did the Danes have allies in the Danelaw, but now Anglo-Saxons across England could join Edgar against the Normans.

The combined army marched on York, reaching it on 21 September. In attempting to clear houses out of the way of defences, the Norman defenders accidentally set fire to the city. Perhaps because their defences were damaged in the fire, they went out to meet the Anglo–Danish army and were cut to pieces. An estimated 3,000 Normans were killed, both castles were destroyed and all the plunder was carried back to the Danish fleet. William's control of England was under enormous pressure.

The Normans held on, however. They were able to do this for two main reasons:

1 William's leadership: when William led troops into a rebel area, the rebels scattered.
2 Instead of pressing south to challenge Norman control directly, the Anglo-Danish army split up.

After victory in York, the Danes sailed across the Humber to the coast of Lincolnshire, difficult to access by land because of swamps. The Anglo-Saxon rebels scattered. As William's army set about hunting them down, news came in of a series of other rebellions in Devon and the earldoms of Shrewsbury and Chester (see Figure 2.6).

But as soon as William and his troops arrived in a rebel area, the rebels disappeared. Once William left for another rebel hotspot, the rebellion flared up again. Meanwhile, William could not attack the Danes by land (because of the swamps), and attacking Vikings at sea would be foolish since the Normans had no fleet and were far less experienced sailors than the Danes.

It was clear to William that the Danes were biding their time, perhaps waiting for Norman military strength to be exhausted dealing with the constant outbreaks of rebellion.

Activities ?

1 Select evidence from this information about the rebellions in the North to use in an argument about the importance of castles in securing Norman control of England.
2 Explain who you think was the bigger threat to William: the Anglo-Saxons or the Danes.

William's solution

It was the Danes who represented the major threat to William: he had routed the English rebels several times, but the North was half-Danish and there was a very serious danger of a Danish invasion being welcomed in Northumbria. In response, William did the following:

- He paid the Danes a large amount of money to leave. This is what Anglo-Saxon leaders had done in the past, although the Danes had then always come back for more.
- He embarked on a campaign of total destruction known as the 'Harrying* of the North' in the winter of 1069–70.

The features of the Harrying included burning crops in the fields, destroying seed crops and killing livestock to make life impossible in the region. It also ensured that, if the Danes came back, there would be nothing to support them and no people to help them. Thousands died of starvation as a result. The consequences of the Harrying of the North are discussed on page 58.

Key term

Harrying*

An archaic (old) word meaning to lay waste to something, to devastate it.

Hereward the Wake and rebellion at Ely, 1070–71

The return of the Danes

In 1070, a Danish fleet returned to England, this time with King Sweyn himself as its leader. Instead of heading to Northumbria, Sweyn set up on the Isle of Ely, in the middle of the Fens in East Anglia.

Extend your knowledge

The Ely Fens

The Fens is a marshy region in the east of England. It was very difficult, treacherous ground, where local knowledge of safe paths was essential. In 1070, Ely was surrounded by water and swamp; an excellent defensive location for the Danes and rebels.

Hereward the Wake

East Anglia was part of the Danelaw and Sweyn made alliances with the local people, including a rebel leader called Hereward the Wake. Hereward was a local thegn who had been exiled under Edward the Confessor, had fought as a mercenary for Flanders and who came back around 1069 to find his lands had been seized and given to a Norman. At the same time, the Archbishop of Peterborough, near to Ely, who may have been Hereward's lord, was replaced by a Norman called Turold. Using the treacherous Fenland terrain to his advantage, Hereward had been fighting a guerrilla war* against the Normans with other East Anglia rebels.

Exam-style question, Section B

Describe **two** features of the rebellions in the North, 1069.

4 marks

Exam tip

This question is about key features and characteristics. Remember to provide supporting information for each feature. For example: the main rebellion combined Anglo-Saxon and Danish forces, led by Edgar Aethling and Asbjorn of Denmark.

Key term

Guerrilla war*

When small bands attack a larger force by surprise and then disappear back into the local population. It is a modern term.

Source B

This photo shows Ely cathedral today when the river is flooded; you can see that Ely is on higher ground surrounded by swampy wetland. The Normans started building Ely cathedral in 1083.

The threat	Approach to threat	Outcome
Danish invasion	Pay the Danes to go away. Harrying of the North to remove support for future invasions.	Rebels easier to defeat without Danish support.
'Guerrilla warfare' from the rebels – avoiding open battle	Rapid response to outbreaks of rebellion. William also used trusted followers to keep areas under control while he led larger forces to deal with serious unrest. Troops searched out rebel hideouts. Castles re-imposed control. Harrying of the North made areas uninhabitable for rebels (and everyone else).	The experience of stamping out rebellions made William decide that the Anglo-Saxon aristocracy needed to be removed from power: a permanent solution to prevent more rebellion in the future.
Discontent from troops and followers	William's knights and his mercenary troops complained about the constant marching, especially in winter. William's strong leadership got them through, together with promises of more rewards.	More land was taken from Anglo-Saxons; money for his troops came from taxes and was taken from the Church.
Edgar as the 'real' king – a stronger claim to the throne	William carried out royal ceremonies so people could see him as king. For example, he left York after the first uprising so that he could celebrate Easter at Winchester: the ancient centre of royal power.	Many English people followed William against the rebels: William's armies were levied from English shires and some thegns defended towns against rebels.

The attack on Peterborough and fall of Ely

The Danes and Hereward raided Peterborough Abbey together. Hereward wanted to stop its riches falling into the hands of the Normans. Unfortunately, the Danes promptly sailed off with the treasure back to Denmark. Hereward was joined by Morcar and his men. As the Normans advanced, led by William, Hereward and Morcar prepared to defend the Isle of Ely. The Normans managed to capture Ely, possibly by bribing local monks to show them a safe way through the marshes. However it was done, Ely was captured, along with Morcar. Hereward escaped, and was not heard of again.

Extend your knowledge

The fates of the earls
Morcar was imprisoned by William for the rest of his life. Edwin, Earl of Mercia, was dead by 1071. His own men had turned on him and killed him. William took the brothers' lands.

The end of the Anglo-Saxon rebellions

The defeat of the rebels at Ely marked the end of the large-scale Anglo-Saxon rebellions. At around the same time as Hereward fled Ely, it seems that Eadric the Wild also abandoned his rebellion against the Marcher earls, possibly after being beaten in battle at Shrewsbury. How had William approached the threats to his control, and what outcomes did these approaches have?

Summary

- The years 1068–71 involved rebellion due mainly to resentment over land.
- Edwin and Morcar's revolt in 1068 collapsed quickly.
- The Northern rebellions of 1069 and Ely in 1070–71 were very serious because of the involvement of Danish invasion fleets.
- William's brutal tactics were successful in ending the Anglo-Saxon rebellions.

Checkpoint

Strengthen

S1 Identify two causes of Anglo-Saxon resistance in the period 1068–71.

S2 How do you think William's attitude to Earl Edwin changed from 1066 to 1071? Draw a graph, with time along the bottom axis from 1066 to 1071 and William's feelings on the vertical axis, ranging from very positive at the top to very negative at the bottom.

S3 Describe two ways in which William successfully dealt with Anglo-Saxon rebellions.

Challenge

C1 Explain why the Anglo-Saxon earls and Edgar were not able to win against William.

C2 To what extent do you agree that William did want to include the Anglo-Saxon earls in the way he ruled England? Develop at least two points for each side of your argument.

C3 William made a law that meant a whole community was responsible for any murder of a Norman. What does this law suggest about resistance to Norman rule in England?

How confident do you feel about your answers to these questions? If you are not sure you answered them well, try the activity below.

Activity ?

Many similar events happened in a short period of time in 1068–71. Create your own timeline for the period to help get the events straight and identify the links between each event.

The Harrying of the North, 1069–70

Reasons for the Harrying of the North

William is reported to have regretted his decision to lay waste to the North for the rest of his life. We can assume that he was acting as much out of fury and frustration as cool strategic thinking.

- Earl Robert Cumin and his men had been slaughtered, and thousands more Normans were killed at York, for which William swore revenge.

- The northern rebels were refusing to meet him in open battle, scattering as he advanced, then launching attacks on his men as soon as he went away to deal with rebellions elsewhere. William's response was to make it impossible for anyone, rebels included, to be able to stay in the area.

- William had perhaps not previously realised how different the North was from southern England; how much they resented rule from the South, and how closely many identified with their Danish heritage. The North clearly required different tactics.

- The rebellions in the North were triggering rebellions elsewhere in the country; it was not possible for William to continue dragging troops from one hotspot to another.

- The threat of Danish invasion was very serious and threatened everything William had achieved in England. At the same time, Normandy faced a serious rebellion in neighbouring Maine. William prioritised England, despite the threat to Normandy.

Key term

Genocide*

A deliberate and organised attempt to exterminate an entire group of people.

These reasons all influenced the Harrying of the North. Although these were violent times, it is important to say that, for contemporary chroniclers, the Harrying was extraordinarily violent and brutal. Some modern day historians have labelled it as genocide*.

That said, the Harrying of the North was similar to the destruction in Wessex at the start of the Norman invasion; William's troops had also destroyed everything in their path as they marched around London. But the Harrying of the North was on a much larger scale and so thorough that it created a disaster zone for many years after.

Source A

When the Normans landed on the south coast, they burned down houses in Wessex, as shown in this scene from the Bayeux Tapestry.

Immediate impacts of the Harrying

The area that William's troops laid waste to stretched from the River Humber to the River Tees (with similar destruction in rebel areas of Staffordshire and parts of Shropshire). (See Figure 2.6 on page 53.) The immediate impacts were similar to a natural disaster. It is thought that as many as 100,000 people died.

- Without any crops to live on, or livestock to slaughter and eat, and with little protection from the cold winter after their homes were burned down, people starved or froze to death.
- William's troops also destroyed seeds for the next year's crops, so there was no hope of starting again. Thousands of refugees fled the region.
- There were reports of cannibalism and of people selling themselves into slavery for food.

Source B

Chronicler Symeon of Durham recorded the events.

It was horrible to observe, in houses, streets and roads, human corpses rotting... For no-one survived to cover them with earth, all having perished by the sword and starvation, or left the land of their fathers because of hunger.

Long-term impacts of the Harrying of the North, 1069–87

The Harrying of the North was a deliberate attempt to remove the people of Northumbria as a threat to Norman control. Although Malcolm III launched attacks after 1071, there were no further uprisings in Northumbria.

The Domesday Book was a record of landholding in England based on detailed local surveys ordered by William in 1085. The surveys recorded what land had been producing in 1066 compared to 1086. What it showed in Yorkshire, the centre of the Harrying of the North, was that the region had not recovered almost 20 years later.

- Sixty per cent of Yorkshire was classed as waste and without livestock. Waste meant there was no economic activity going on that could be taxed.

- There were between 80,000 and 150,000 fewer people than in January 1066.

The Harrying of the North also had other long-term impacts.

- Removing large numbers of Anglo–Danes from Northumbria had a lasting impact on the chances of Danish invasion. Sweyn's choice of Ely for the attack of 1070–71 suggests Northumbria was no longer suitable.
- For William and Norman control of England, the Harrying of the North was a turning point. Instead of winning over the Anglo-Saxon aristocracy, William now decided to replace them.
- The Harrying of the North was widely criticised, including by the pope. William devoted much time and money to the Church for the rest of his reign in order to make amends for what he had done.

Activity ?

How would a modern-day news report cover the Harrying of the North? Write a script for a report involving the following: a news anchor role to introduce the story and set it in context; a reporter role, giving an eye-witness account of events; short interviews with a Northern refugee and a Norman soldier, and a statement from William's government.

Exam-style question, Section B

'The main reason for the Harrying of the North was to prevent another Danish invasion'.

How far do you agree? Explain your answer.

You may use the following in your answer:

- Robert Cumin
- Danelaw.

You **must** also use information of your own. **16 marks**

Exam tip

This is a question about causation (reasons for). Include your own information, as well as arguments prompted by the bullet points, otherwise it really limits how successful your answer can be.

Changes in landownership from Anglo-Saxon to Norman, 1066–87

A landholding revolution

Between 1066 and 1087, the Normans replaced the Anglo-Saxons as landholders. By 1087:

- over half of all the land in England was held by about 190 tenants-in-chief*. Only two of them were Anglo-Saxons (Thurkill of Arden and Colswein of Lincoln)
- a quarter of the land was held by the Church. Normans held most senior Church positions
- the king's royal estates made up one-fifth of the land
- less than 5% of the land was still held by Anglo-Saxon aristocrats, typically in small estates.

Key term

Tenants-in-chief*

The large landholders of Norman England who held their land directly from the king.

Extend your knowledge

The great tenants

Half the land held by the 190 tenants-in-chief was in the hands of just 11 men. These included Odo of Bayeux, Robert of Mortain and William FitzOsbern: all Norman nobles and William's relatives. But William also gave large grants of land to men from more modest backgrounds, such as William de Warenne, who became Earl of Surrey. The 11 also included loyal non-Normans: Allan the Red from Brittany, for example.

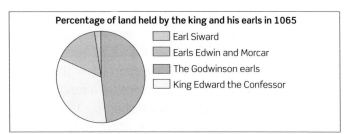

Percentage of land held by the king and his earls in 1065

- Earl Siward
- Earls Edwin and Morcar
- The Godwinson earls
- King Edward the Confessor

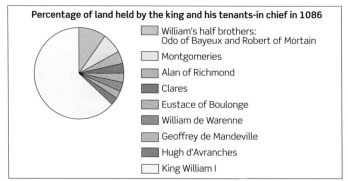

Percentage of land held by the king and his tenants-in chief in 1086

- William's half brothers: Odo of Bayeux and Robert of Mortain
- Montgomeries
- Alan of Richmond
- Clares
- Eustace of Boulonge
- William de Warenne
- Geoffrey de Mandeville
- Hugh d'Avranches
- King William I

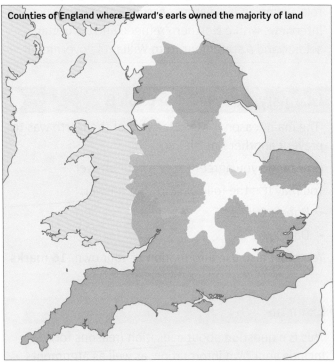

Counties of England where Edward's earls owned the majority of land

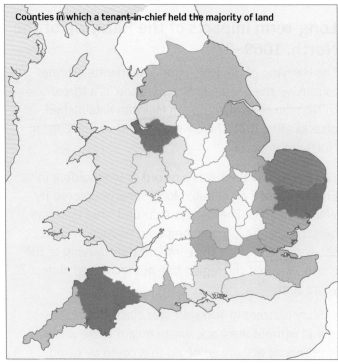

Counties in which a tenant-in-chief held the majority of land

Figure 2.7 The change in landownership between 1066 and 1086.

Landownership and rebellion

The rebellions of 1068, 1069 and 1070–71 showed William that the Anglo-Saxon earls could not be trusted. He took their lands and granted them to his followers, being careful not to give anyone, even his closest followers, too much land. Land was power – it provided revenues and fighting men. The Anglo-Saxon earls had been too powerful and had challenged the king.

Before 1066, there were around 4,000 thegns in England whose landholdings gave them significant status in society. The rebellions showed that, if earls rebelled, so did their thegns. Also, Hereward the Wake and Eadric the Wild were both powerful thegns who led rebellions of their own. By 1087, these 4,000 thegns were no longer a threat. Their Anglo-Saxon lords had almost all been replaced by Normans and most thegns had been forced into being dependent on Normans for the small amount of land that they were still allowed to hold on to.

How did Anglo-Saxons lose their land?

Redistribution of land from Anglo-Saxons to their new masters happened in three main ways. Two of these ways were legal, which was important to William's claims to being a just and fair king.

1) By forfeit*

The king owned all the land in his kingdom, so if anyone acted against the king, his or her lands could be forfeited. William made his followers the 'heirs' of Anglo-Saxons who had forfeited their land. This process continued all the way through William's reign, and included lands forfeited from rebellious Norman earls in 1075.

> **Key term**
>
> **Forfeit***
>
> To lose something as a punishment for committing a crime or bad action.

2) New earldoms

William created new earldoms and other blocks of territory that he granted to his followers. These blocks were put together from the forfeited holdings of several different previous owners. These were created to defend trouble spots. The Marcher earldoms are a good example of this.

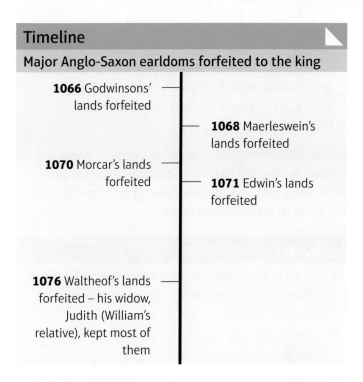

Timeline

Major Anglo-Saxon earldoms forfeited to the king

1066 Godwinsons' lands forfeited

1068 Maerleswein's lands forfeited

1070 Morcar's lands forfeited

1071 Edwin's lands forfeited

1076 Waltheof's lands forfeited – his widow, Judith (William's relative), kept most of them

> **Extend your knowledge**
>
> **An example of forfeiting**
> William sent a writ to the abbot of Bury St Edmunds, which ordered him to hand over the land of his men who had fought for Harold and died at Hastings.

3) Land grabs

This was the illegal way in which Anglo-Saxons lost their land to Normans. There were both straightforward thefts and seizures of land and corrupt dealings that left Anglo-Saxons with less land than before. Norman sheriffs were particularly notorious for this sort of exploitation. (See Chapter 3 for more detail.)

Changes in landholding after 1071

Before the rebellions, William had been able to put Normans in control of Godwinson lands in the South and West; now he could do the same for forfeited lands throughout Mercia, East Anglia and the North. William also changed the way he granted out the land to increase Norman control.

- Before 1071, what an Anglo-Saxon held was passed on to Norman 'heirs' wherever it was in the country. That meant landholders often held land in many different regions.

- After 1071, William consolidated more blocks of territory. These were much better for imposing control because there was a single strong authority in the area. For example, Earl Edwin's Yorkshire holdings were used to create the castlery and lordship of Richmond.

Before 1071, therefore, William was keen to present himself as keeping to Anglo-Saxon law and traditions. After 1071, that illusion was replaced by practical solutions to maintaining control.

Activities ?

1. Link these together in a sentence that explains a change in landownership: Godwinsons + forfeit + tenants-in-chief.

2. Two old thegns meet in 1072. Role-play their conversation about the Normans.

3. Explain why changing who controlled the land reduced the chance of Anglo-Saxon revolt post-1071.

Changes in how land was held

There were important differences between Anglo-Saxon and Norman England in how landownership worked. Under the Normans, tenure* became much less secure. This was deliberate. It made tenants more dependent on their lords and lessened the chance of revolt.

Key term

Tenure*

'To hold' in Latin – it is a short, but precise, way of talking about landholding and landownership.

Anglo-Saxon landholding

By Edward the Confessor's time, there were lots of different types of tenure, including:

- **Bookland:** lords granted out land to their followers, who were given a charter (a document) to show their right to the land. This right to the land could be passed on to heirs or sold to others.

- **Leases:** land was loaned to someone for money. It was loaned for a set period of time. This could be a long time, for example: three generations.

Both types of land carried duties with it, like the fyrd obligation (every five hides = one soldier). And geld tax was also charged on both types of land.

- If someone failed to carry out their obligations or failed to pay their tax, they could lose their land.

- When a new thegn took over land (after the old thegn's death), they had to pay a tax to their lord.

Landholding under the Normans

Landownership in Norman England had some similarities to and some differences from Anglo-Saxon landownership:

- There was only one landowner – the king. William owned all the land. Regardless of any previous agreements, everyone now only had tenure from the king.

- Anglo-Saxon landholders usually had to redeem the land they held back from William. That meant paying William money for the right to keep using their own land. This was unpopular.

- When William granted land to his followers, they did not have to redeem it. However, if they died without an heir, the land went back to the king. If there was an heir, then the heir had to pay a tax to the king when he inherited the land. Landholders acting against the king could lose their land.

William was very powerful under this new system. Although there were similarities to the Anglo-Saxon system, William enforced the laws much more strictly. If people did not do as the king wished, they could lose their lands and be left with nothing.

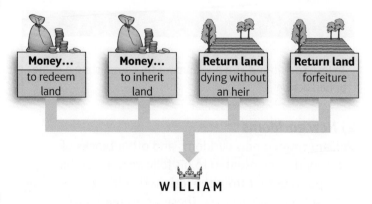

Figure 2.8 Changes to the land holding system reinforced William's control as king.

Landholding under the tenants-in-chief

It wasn't only the king who had this power. His tenants-in-chief had a lot of power, too. When they took over new lands, all the thegns there gained a new lord.

- The tenant-in-chief was allowed to reallocate land when a thegn died. Because the tenants-in-chief had their own followers to reward, they could make their followers 'heirs' to the thegn's land.
- They could dispossess thegns who acted against them or failed to fulfil their obligations to their lord.

Thegns might cling on to some land, therefore, but their way of life was completely changed. Many left England to work as mercenaries in Europe. Those that stayed had to be obedient vassals* to their new lords if they wanted to survive. Although resentment over this new system was a reason for the revolts, once the revolts were suppressed it became a strong controlling factor.

Changes for the peasants

Landholders did not farm the land themselves; that was done by the peasants. Life hadn't been easy for them under Anglo-Saxon rule, but it does seem as though the new tenants-in-chief were keener to get more revenue from their lands and that meant even harder times for the peasants.

In Anglo-Saxon England, ceorls didn't own the land they worked, but they leased it from the lord and were independent farmers. Although there are records that show some ceorls kept the same landholdings in the same way as before 1066, in most cases the evidence shows that these free peasants became rarer and rarer. The new lords made the peasants work for them and reduced their independence.

> **Key term**
>
> **Vassal***
> Someone who held their land in return for services to their Norman lord.

> **Extend your knowledge**
>
> **Land seizures**
> Victims of land seizures did appeal and, in a few cases, were able to get some land back in compensation. Some tenants were able to prove landholding rights if they had charters showing their right to the land. But the king was unlikely to allow this where there had been revolts or resistance.

> **Exam-style question, Section B**
>
> Explain why changes in landownership made resistance to Norman control less likely after 1071.
>
> You may use the following in your answer:
> - tenants-in-chief
> - thegns.
>
> You **must** also use information of your own. **12 marks**

> **Exam tip**
>
> This question is about causation. Your answer should combine your knowledge of key features about the period (e.g. how landownership changed) with your analysis of the reasons why changes in landownership were linked to increased control.

> **Source B**
>
> This picture of ploughing is from an 11th-century calendar, which was probably created in Winchester. Under the Normans, most peasants came to depend on their lord instead of paying rent and farming their land independently.

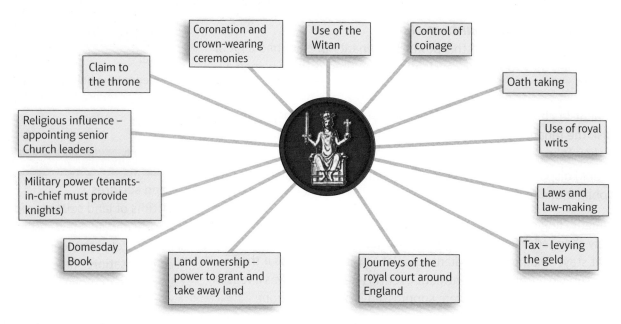

Figure 2.9 The powers of King William I. The image in the middle is a representation of William's royal seal.

Maintaining royal power

Military strength

The main way that William maintained his power as king of England was through his military strength, his skill as a military leader and his ruthlessness: the brutal way in which he crushed rebellion. Anglo-Saxons had great respect for kings who were great warriors and his skill, ruthlessness and luck in battle would have proved to many in England that he was favoured by God. So, as well as keeping him as king by crushing his enemies, William's military power also gave him legitimacy as leader amongst the English. Many Anglo-Saxons joined William's armies against the rebels.

William's military brilliance made him an awesome conqueror, but he wanted to rule England as a king. In order to do that he needed to be recognised by the English as their *legitimate* ruler, especially as others had their own right to the throne, such as Edgar Aethling.

The legitimate successor

William's claim to the throne – that Edward the Confessor promised it to him – was continually stressed throughout his reign. William's right to be king was also explained through his being a relation of Edward's (his cousin) and that, because Harold had broken holy oaths to William and falsely claimed the throne, God had chosen William to defeat Harold and put things right.

Activity ?
Congratulations: you have invaded another country and been crowned by its archbishop. What actions will you now take to promote your image as the rightful monarch? And why would you need to bother, when you have military superiority over the natives?

Royal ceremonies

At his coronation, William swore to preserve Edward the Confessor's laws, protect the Church and rule with equal justice for all his subjects. Then he received the crown, the symbol of royal power, and was anointed with sacred oil, which confirmed him as being appointed king by the will of God.

William instituted a new custom of being seen wearing his crown three times a year, at which point he also discussed the business of the realm with the important men of his kingdom (which was referred to as his Witan). The three times were at the most important times of the Christian calendar (over Easter and Christmas) and also in different important places in the kingdom (Winchester, Westminster, Gloucester). He also wore his crown in a ceremony in the ruins of York on Christmas day 1069, having put down Edgar the Aethling's rebellion.

Coinage and writs

William took control of the minting of coins. The treasury remained at Winchester. The coins had an image of William on them, as did his royal seal. The seal was attached to the king's writs (official documents and proclamations). It showed William on his throne on one side and as a knight, mounted on a horse, on the other. Normandy did not have a system like writs, but William clearly found them very effective as a way of maintaining royal power across the whole country.

Journeys around England

In medieval times, the regions of England were very different from each other, with few people ever travelling very far from home. To maintain his royal power in each region, the king needed to be seen there, otherwise his authority would feel very far away. The king and royal court travelled around the country, meeting with important local families and officials. The arrival of the king in a region was a very splendid occasion – unless, of course, he was leading an army to crush a rebellion.

Owning the land

The system of landownership that made William the owner of all the land in England was very significant in increasing and maintaining his royal power. Now everyone who held land was connected in a chain of tenants and tenants-in-chief directly to the king. This connection was much stronger than in Edward the Confessor's time. William was constantly exercising this royal power: taking back land from rebels or those who had died without heirs, granting it out again to followers, hearing complaints and making judgements about how his land was being used.

Oath-taking

Oaths were taken very seriously and William held oath-taking ceremonies in which all men would swear to serve him loyally. The biggest was in 1086, when another great Viking invasion seemed imminent. The ceremony was held at Salisbury and every landholder of any kind of importance, whoever they were tenants of, came and swore their loyalty to the king. This must have involved hundreds of men, possibly thousands.

Summary

- Anglo-Saxon resistance convinced William that sharing power would not work.
- The Harrying of the North demonstrated the extent of William's ruthlessness.
- Changing landownership made thegns poorer and more dependent on their new lords.
- Military skill and strength was the foundation of William's royal power.

Checkpoint

Strengthen

S1 Describe one immediate impact of the Harrying of the North and one long-term impact.

S2 Imagine you are a tenant-in-chief hoping to convince more Normans to come over to live on your new estates in England. Create a poster explaining the advantages.

S3 Compare the information about William's royal power here with the information about Anglo-Saxon kings on pages 11–12. What are the similarities and differences?

Challenge

C1 William had laid waste to plenty of English towns and villages before 1069–70. Was the Harrying of the North any different? Support the points in your argument with examples.

C2 Explain how changes in landownership made Anglo-Saxon rebellions less likely to occur.

Activity

When we read information from a book, website or our notes, it is tempting to think 'yes, I know all this' or 'I get what this is about'. A great way to **really** find out what you do remember and how much you actually understand is to try and tell someone else about it. Try explaining how William retained control of England to a partner. If there are any gaps in what you can explain, go back to your notes and fill them in.

2.4 Revolt of the Earls, 1075

The conspirators

The revolt of 1075 was different from the rebellions of 1068–71 because it included Normans rebelling against William and Anglo-Saxons defending their king. For that reason, the revolt of 1075 is sometimes known as 'the revolt of the Norman Earls' but it was more complex than that.

The rebellion's leader was Ralph de Gael, Earl of East Anglia. Ralph plotted with Roger de Breteuil, Earl of Hereford and Waltheof, Earl of Northumbria to overthrow William and divide the kingdom into three between them. In order to add muscle to their plan, Ralph contacted the Danes for help, who put together an impressive invasion fleet led by Cnut, son of King Sweyn. The rebels also had support from Normandy's rivals, Brittany and France. Both states wanted to weaken Normandy.

To understand the revolt properly, it helps to look at each of the three main men involved in more detail.

Roger de Breteuil, Earl of Hereford

Roger was the son of William FitzOsbern, lord of Breteuil in Normandy and the same man that William had rewarded so lavishly in 1066: making him Earl of Hereford, a Marcher earldom with extensive powers. Roger had succeeded his father as Earl in 1071, after FitzOsbern died abroad.

Waltheof, Earl of Northumbria

Waltheof was the son of Earl Siward. When Siward had died in 1055 and Edward had made Tostig Earl of Northumbria, Waltheof was too young to challenge him. By 1065, he was Earl of Northamptonshire and, after submitting to William in 1066, he was allowed to stay as earl. In 1069, he was part of the rebellions in the North, but he submitted again to William and was pardoned, unlike his cousin, Gospatric. When Gospatric fled England in 1072, William made Waltheof Earl of Northumbria — perhaps as a gesture of reconciliation* over the Harrying of the North.

Ralph de Gael, Earl of East Anglia

Ralph was the son of an Anglo-Norman who had served Edward the Confessor and then been rewarded with lands in East Anglia by William (probably Gyrth Godwinson's land) in 1066. Ralph's mother was from Brittany and Ralph was brought up there. When his father died, Ralph succeeded him as Earl of East Anglia, in around 1069. In 1075, Ralph married the sister of Roger de Breteuil.

Key term

Reconciliation*

To find ways for former enemies to forgive each other.

Reasons for the revolt

Resentments   **Opportunities**

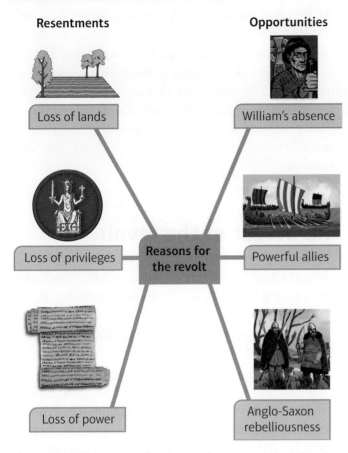

- Loss of lands
- Loss of privileges
- Loss of power

- William's absence
- Powerful allies
- Anglo-Saxon rebelliousness

Reasons for the revolt

Figure 2.10 The reasons for the revolt were connected to the earls' resentments and opportunities.

Of all three men, it is Roger who seems the least likely rebel. His father had been so essential to William's conquest and to establishing control of England that Roger's loyalty must have been assumed. However, Roger objected to the fact that the amount of land he had control over was less than that granted to his father. William had clearly taken the opportunity to reduce the power of the de Bretueils now that FitzOsbern was dead. Also, William had introduced his own sheriffs into the Marcher earldoms, where before the earls had controlled everything for themselves. This loss of authority frustrated Roger. It was a very similar problem to that experienced by the Anglo-Saxon earls and it explains why the plan of the rebels in 1075 was to split the country into three great estates.

Ralph's motives are not well known, but we can assume that he too resented a loss of power and wealth compared to his father's holdings.

As for Waltheof, the reasons for his involvement are clouded by his actions. Perhaps he played both sides, using his contacts in Denmark to make the chances of success greater, then choosing to inform when it looked less likely that the revolt would succeed.

Exam-style question, Section B ⚪

Describe **two** features of the Revolt of the Earls in 1075.   **4 marks**

Exam tip ⚪

This question is about identifying key features. Your answer should identify each feature and give some supporting information about it.

The events of the revolt

Ralph's wedding feast

When Ralph married Emma, Roger de Breteuil's sister, there was a very big wedding feast. Important bishops, abbots, earls and magnates* were invited, including Waltheof. It was at the wedding feast that Ralph and Roger told Waltheof of their plans. With his background of rebellion against William, the last surviving major Anglo-Saxon earl must have appeared an ideal co-conspirator. Between the three of them, their lands stretched from west to east and from the far north to the Midlands.

Key term ▸

Magnate*

The historical term for a great man, an important and influential figure.

Ralph and Roger anticipated support in their revolt from Anglo-Saxons and from the Danish fleet. Possibly Waltheof was a key recruit for gaining this support: the last surviving Anglo-Saxon earl, with strong contacts with King Sweyn in Denmark, too. The rebels had also timed their revolt for a point when William was in Normandy, with Archbishop Lanfranc in charge of England.

The plan unfolds

Unfortunately for the earls, their revolt did not get widespread Anglo-Saxon support and the Danish fleet arrived too late. The revolt was defeated before it really began:

- Waltheof thought better of getting involved and informed Archbishop Lanfranc. Lanfranc sent men to find out what was happening in the earldoms of Hereford and East Anglia. They reported that the rebels were strengthening the defences of their castles and building up troops ready for a combined attack.

- Lanfranc wrote letters to Roger, trying to convince him not to take this drastic step. He reminded Roger of how loyal his father had been to William, and how Roger should follow his father's example. When these had no effect, he used the power of excommunication* to cut Roger off from the Church until he gave up his plans for revolt.

- Meanwhile, preparations were being made to counter the revolt. In the West, Bishop Wulfstan of Worcester and the abbot of Evesham used their troops to prevent Roger crossing the Severn River, bottling him up in Herefordshire. The same thing happened in the East, with the Normans and Anglo-Saxons joining together to stop Ralph from breaking out of his earldom of East Anglia. The Anglo-Saxon Chronicle for 1075 describes the situation for Ralph in Source A.

- William then returned to England. Around this point, the Danes arrived – a huge fleet of 200 ships. But they were too late to help the revolt. The Danish fleet could have stretched Norman defences beyond their limit. However, the Anglo-Saxon Chronicle states that the Danes' two leaders, Cnut and Earl Hakon, 'dared not join battle with William' himself. Rather than invade, the fleet raided up the east coast, as usual, and sacked York cathedral before going home again.

Key term

Excommunication*

Cutting off someone from the Church community so that they are unable to confess their sins before they die, which people believed would prevent them from ever going to heaven. The idea was not to punish someone permanently, but to convince them to act properly so they could then re-join the Church.

Source A

The Worcester version of the Anglo-Saxon Chronicle for the year 1075 (adapted).

Ralph tried to move his troops from East Anglia out for battle, but the garrisons of the Norman castles which were in England, together with the inhabitants of the country, opposed them and did everything they could to stop them, so that nothing was accomplished and Ralph only just managed to escape to his ships at Norwich.

The defeat of the revolt

- While Ralph escaped to Brittany, his wife, Emma (Roger's sister), held out in Norwich castle, which had very strong defences, until she could make a deal that guaranteed her and their followers safe passage to Brittany. Ralph's rebellious Breton followers were either blinded or banished.

- Waltheof fled abroad. William tricked him into thinking that he would be forgiven if he came back and submitted to the king. When Waltheof did come back, he was imprisoned. Waltheof might have hoped that his actions in reporting the rebellion would count in his favour, but William must have run out of patience with him, as he was executed in May 1076 at Winchester.

- William imprisoned Roger for life (like Morcar).

- William then travelled back to Normandy and attacked Ralph's castle at Dol. Facing stiff resistance, plus troops sent to aid Brittany from France, William had to retreat. Military victory proved far harder for William to achieve back home than in England.

Extend your knowledge

Norman military power

Although William's knights and castles gave him military superiority in England, in Normandy he was fighting against enemies with knights and castles of their own. New tactics were being developed at this time - charging other knights with couched lances and siege technology against castles.

Activities ?

1 Create a storyboard for a short film about the events and defeat of the Revolt of the Earls.

2 In groups, role-play the plotting at Ralph's wedding feast between the three earls. Each earl should give a speech about their own grievances against William.

3 Put together a short biography of Waltheof, including his earldoms, his relationship with William (including his marriage to Judith) and his involvement in rebellion against William. Decide how justified William was in his final punishment of Waltheof.

THINKING HISTORICALLY   Cause and Consequence (4a&b)

Fragile history

Nothing that happens is inevitable. Sometimes things happen due to the actions of an individual or chance events that no one anticipated. Something could have altered or someone could have chosen differently, bringing about a very different outcome. What actually occurred in the past did happen, but it did not have to be like that.

Work on your own and answer the questions below. When you have answered the questions, discuss the answers in a group. Then have a class vote.

Perceived reasons for the rebellions in the North, 1069

State of affairs	Event	Development	Event	Trigger event
Anglo-Saxon leaders plan attacks from Scotland, Danish fleet is assembled for invasion	The massacre of Robert Cumin and his troops	Anglo-Saxon resentment over Norman land grabs, brutality and repression	Combined Anglo–Danish army destroys Norman forces in York	Fire in York, set accidentally by Norman forces, weakens Norman defences

1 Consider the massacre of Robert Cumin and his troops and the Anglo-Saxon resentment of Normans at the time.

   a How did the massacre affect the leaders of Anglo-Saxon resistance, especially Edgar Aethling?

   b Had there been no massacre, would the rebellions in the North still have happened?

   c What other aspects of the situation in 1070s Norman England could have been affected had Robert Cumin succeeded in becoming earl in the North?

2 Consider the planned attacks from Scotland and Denmark, the combined attack on York and the accidental fire that meant the Normans' defences were weakened.

   a How important is the planned Danish invasion as a causal factor of the two events?

   b What might have happened had the Danes changed their plans and the invasion not happened?

3 What other consequences came about as a result of the information in the table? Try to identify at least one consequence for each.

4 Choose one reason from the table. How might the rebellions in the North have developed differently if this factor had not been present?

The effects of the revolt

The Revolt of the Earls suggests some significant changes had happened in Norman England:

- William now needed to be careful of his own earls. Ambition, and resentment of the power William kept to himself, was at the heart of Roger and Ralph's revolt. From this point on, rebellion against William and his sons came from the Norman magnates.

- Anglo-Saxons joined the loyal Normans in stopping the revolts from spreading. The involvement of Anglo-Saxon men like Bishop Wulfstan also suggests that some Anglo-Saxons now supported the Normans.

However, there is no evidence of William reversing his policy of eliminating the Anglo-Saxon aristocracy. The execution of Waltheof suggests one effect of the revolt was that William now stamped down harder than ever on any sign of Anglo-Saxon rebellion, especially when it involved links to Denmark.

- The failure of the planned Danish invasion in 1075 was, in fact, the end of the Viking threat to England. But William did not know this. When there was another invasion threat from Denmark in 1085, William took extraordinary measures to boost England's defences (see page 00). This suggests that William saw the events of 1075 as very threatening, meaning a tight grip had to be maintained.

Summary

- The Revolt of the Earls in 1075 was linked to William's policy of reducing the size of earldoms and the power of earls. He wanted to be much stronger than his earls.
- The revolt was extremely threatening for William. It linked three powerful earls, a large invasion force of Danes, and support from Brittany and France.
- The revolt failed because Lanfranc organised counter-measures, Anglo-Saxons supported William and William's reputation (and the failure of the earls' revolt) stopped the Danes from doing more than raiding the eastern coast.

Checkpoint

Strengthen

S1 Who were the earls who led the Revolt of the Earls and where were they earls of?

S2 William had originally given Marcher earls like William FitzOsbern much greater powers than other earls. Name three of these greater powers.

S3 Identify three reasons for the Revolt of the Earls and three reasons for its defeat.

Challenge

C1 Why do you think William had Waltheof executed? What had changed from Waltheof's previous rebellions?

C2 Which do you think is more significant for Norman control of England: that a Norman rebelled against his king, that Anglo-Saxons fought against the rebels or that the Danish leaders did not want to have to fight William in battle? Explain your choice.

C3 Bishop Wulfstan and Archbishop Lanfranc were both important in preventing the revolt from spreading. Did they achieve this through religious power or through military power?

How confident do you feel about your answers to these questions? If you are not sure you answered them well, try the following activity.

Activity

Point, Evidence, Explain (PEE): use this when you are making your notes, as well as when you are writing something for assessment, because it gets you thinking in the right way. For example: resentment at loss of power and wealth was an important reason for the Revolt of the Earls in 1075. What evidence could you use to back that point up? How could you then explain why it is an important reason? Apply this method to your notes from this section.

Recap: William I in power: securing the kingdom, 1066–87

Recall quiz

1 Who did the Witan first name as king after Harold's death?

2 Where did William receive the submission of the earls?

3 Name the three Marcher earldoms.

4 Name three features of a motte and bailey castle that made them difficult to attack.

5 Who escaped back to Scotland after the revolt of Edwin and Morcar?

6 What did Harrying of the North involve?

7 Name three ways in which land was transferred from Anglo-Saxons to Normans.

8 Name the three earls who plotted against William in 1075.

9 What happened to each of the three earls after their revolt was defeated?

10 Who was in charge in England at the start of the Revolt of the Earls?

Exam-style question, Section B

'William's strategy for ruling England had failed by 1070'.

How far do you agree? Explain your answer.

You may use the following in your answer:

• the submission of the earls
• the Harrying of the North.

You **must** also use information of your own. **16 marks**

Exam tip

This question is about consequence. It requires the weighing of aspects of success and failure to make a judgement.

Activities

1 The spider diagram here has been started off for you – copy it out onto a large sheet of paper and complete it to detail: causes, consequences, features and characteristics.

2 What are three questions about this topic that you would like to know the answer to? For example, what happened to Gospatric? Did Harold have any children and, if so, did they try to recover their lands? How important were women in Anglo-Saxon revolts? Research answers to your three questions for a presentation to the rest of the class.

3 Compare the royal power of William with that of Edward the Confessor. To what extent did William continue the powers of the king rather than change them?

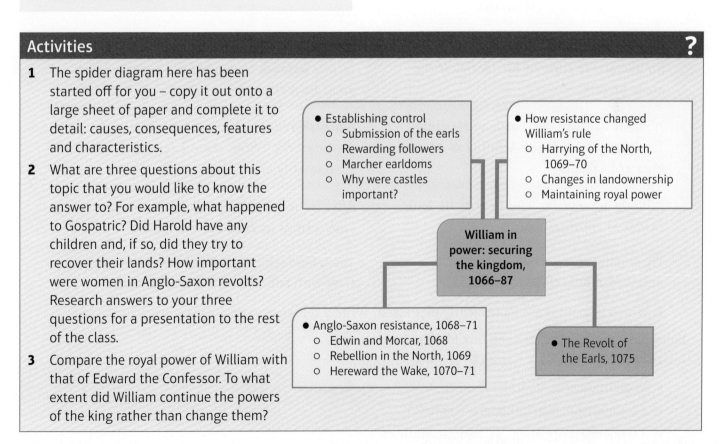

• Establishing control
  ○ Submission of the earls
  ○ Rewarding followers
  ○ Marcher earldoms
  ○ Why were castles important?

• How resistance changed William's rule
  ○ Harrying of the North, 1069–70
  ○ Changes in landownership
  ○ Maintaining royal power

William in power: securing the kingdom, 1066–87

• Anglo-Saxon resistance, 1068–71
  ○ Edwin and Morcar, 1068
  ○ Rebellion in the North, 1069
  ○ Hereward the Wake, 1070–71

• The Revolt of the Earls, 1075

Writing historically: building sentences

Successful historical writing uses a range of sentence structures to achieve clarity, precision and emphasis.

Learning outcomes

By the end of this lesson, you will understand how to:

- use and position subordinate clauses to link ideas with clarity and precision
- manipulate sentence structure to emphasise key ideas.

Definitions

Clause: a group of words or unit of meaning that contains a verb and can form part or all of a sentence.

Single clause sentence: a sentence containing just one clause.

Subordinating conjunction: a word used to link a dependent clause to the main clause of a sentence.

How can I use sentence structure to link my ideas?

When you are explaining and exploring complex events and ideas, you need to show clearly and precisely how they are linked.

1. Compare the two drafts of sentences below, written in response to this exam-style question:

> Explain why William was able to become king of England after the Battle of Hastings. **(12 marks)**

William's use of castle building was key to his success. It ensured his control of the areas he took.	William's castle building was key to his success because it ensured his control of the areas he took.
William had won the Battle of Hastings. The Witan chose Edgar Aethling to become king of England.	Although William had won the Battle of Hastings, the Witan chose Edgar Aethling to become king of England.
William secured the south coast. He built castles at Hastings and Dover.	After he secured the south coast, William built castles at Hastings and Dover.

These points are written in pairs of unlinked, **single clause sentences**.

The relationship between these points is made clear with **subordinating conjunctions**.

2. Which responses are more clearly expressed? Write a sentence or two explaining your answer.

Subordinating conjunctions can link ideas to indicate:

- an explanation: (e.g. 'because', 'as', 'in order that')
- a condition: (e.g. 'if', 'unless')
- a comparison: (e.g. 'although', 'whereas')
- a sequence: (e.g. 'when', 'as', 'before', 'until' etc.)

How can I structure my sentences for clarity and emphasis?

In sentences where ideas are linked with subordinate conjunctions, there is:

- a main clause that gives the central point of the sentence
- a dependent, subordinate clause that adds more information about that central point.

Different sentence structures can alter the emphasis of your writing. Look at these sentences that have been used to introduce responses to the exam-style question on the previous page.

Compare these two versions of the first sentence:

> _Although William had won the Battle of Hastings, the Witan chose Edgar Aethling to become king of England. William's decisions and tactics enabled him to become king instead._

This is the main clause in this sentence

This is a subordinate clause. It is linked to the main clause with a subordinating conjunction.

> _The Witan chose Edgar Aethling to become king of England although William had won the Battle of Hastings. William's decisions and tactics enabled him to become king instead._

3. Which clause is given more emphasis in each version? Explain your answer.

The second sentence in the response above is much shorter than the first sentence:

4. Why do you think the writer chose to make this point in a short sentence? Why does it come after, and not before, the other sentence? Write a sentence or two explaining your ideas.

5. a. Experiment with different ways of sequencing the three pieces of information in the response above, linking all, some, or none of them with subordinating conjunctions:

> _William had won the Battle of Hastings._
>
> _The Witan chose Edgar Aethling to become king of England._
>
> _William's decisions and tactics enabled him to become king instead._

b. Which version links the ideas most clearly? One of yours or the original version? Write a sentence or two explaining your decision.

Improving an answer

6. Now look at the notes below written in response to the exam-style question on the previous page.

> _William's tactics were a key reason for his success._
>
> _He marched on London._
>
> _He ruthlessly harried and burned wherever he went._
>
> _He intimidated the Anglo-Saxons._
>
> _They felt demoralised and incapable of resistance._
>
> _The earls submitted to him at Berkhamstead._
>
> _William had convinced them of his military superiority._

a. Experiment with different ways of sequencing and structuring all the information in sentences. Try to write at least three different versions.

b. Which version gives the best historical account? Write a sentence or two explaining your decision.

03 | Norman England, 1066–88

1066 is the most famous date in English history because of the vital importance of the Norman Conquest. But, how different was Norman England from Anglo-Saxon England?

Historians used to think that the feudal system introduced to England by William I was **very** different from how Anglo-Saxon society was organised. Now, historians have identified as much **continuity** as **change**, although undoubtedly Norman England was governed by different people: the Normans. The way it was governed might have had many similarities to government under Edward the Confessor, but now the purpose of that government was to maintain Norman control and, in particular, boost the power and wealth of the king.

The Domesday Book was the crowning achievement of William's government of England: a record of who owned what and how much they owed the king in taxation. Because it was compiled so quickly, between 1086 and 1087, historians are sure that it was based on detailed Anglo-Saxon government records and the efficient Anglo-Saxon local government system.

Learning outcomes

In this chapter you will find out:

- about the feudal system and changes to the Church by the Normans
- how Norman government worked and what its aims were
- about the Norman aristocracy and the importance of Bishop Odo of Bayeux
- about William I and his sons, and what happened after William died.

3.1 The feudal system and the Church

The feudal system

William needed soldiers to maintain control in England and also to fight battles to defend Normandy. However, an army was enormously expensive: soldiers needed to be paid, men and horses had to be fed, equipment bought and maintained. Knights, in particular, were very costly. The feudal system developed as a way of ensuring that kings had troops without having to pay for them.

The system worked like this. William granted land to his tenants-in-chief to reward them for their loyalty, but the land carried with it a requirement to provide troops when the king needed them. Land with this service obligation was called a fief*. Some fiefs required the holder to provide knights for battle or to garrison the king's castles. Knight service* was for 40 days a year and was unpaid. However, lords had to provide their knights with money to live on during their time serving the king.

The tenants-in-chief granted out land to their followers in order to reward them for their loyalty, but also to provide these service obligations. For example, if a tenant-in-chief had fiefs carrying the obligation to provide ten knights to the king, then he could grant out ten parcels of land to ten of his knights to live on. When the king needed the knights, they would go off to fight for him.

The feudal hierarchy

A hierarchy is when a system is organised into different grades or classes. William made sure that the person at the top of the feudal hierarchy (the king) had ultimate power. The tenants-in-chief were powerful, but they answered to the king. The vassals of the tenants-in-chief, called under-tenants, were much less powerful. They answered to the tenants-in-chief and also swore to be loyal to the king. The peasantry were the ones who did all the actual farming. They had very little power.

Key terms

Fief*

Land held by a vassal in return for service to a lord. Also called a 'feud' (i.e. feudalism).

Knight service*

The duty to provide a mounted knight to the king in exchange for a grant of land. The vassal had to ensure he had the right armour, weapons and equipment to carry out their service.

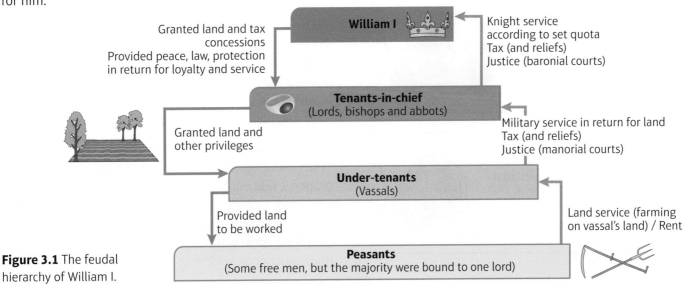

Figure 3.1 The feudal hierarchy of William I.

Granted land and tax concessions
Provided peace, law, protection in return for loyalty and service

William I

Knight service according to set quota
Tax (and reliefs)
Justice (baronial courts)

Tenants-in-chief (Lords, bishops and abbots)

Granted land and other privileges

Military service in return for land
Tax (and reliefs)
Justice (manorial courts)

Under-tenants (Vassals)

Provided land to be worked

Land service (farming on vassal's land) / Rent

Peasants (Some free men, but the majority were bound to one lord)

The role and importance of tenants-in-chief

Tenants-in-chief held their fiefs direct from the king. They had military, social, political and economic roles. There was also a religious element: some were Church leaders: bishops and abbots (these Church tenants-in-chief also had to provide knights to the king).

Military. Expected to fight with him and lead their own band of knights. Also had to defend their own fiefs and put down any opposition to Norman rule.

Social. Provide knights for the king: up to them how they used their land to do it. Thus at the centre of the distribution of land. Organised the transfer of landholding from Anglo-Saxons to Normans.

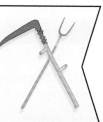

Social. Some had a large number of fiefs, known as an honour or barony*. Each had its own court, judging tenants' cases. All who owed knight service attended, mostly to sort out disputes to do with who was allowed to use which bits of land.

Economically important. They owed the king a share of all the revenue produced by their fiefs and they also kept a share for themselves. Many became extremely wealthy.

Political. Often served on the royal council, advising the king when he requested it. They also had to provide food and accommodation for the king and his court as he travelled the country.

The role and importance of knight service

The Anglo-Saxon word *cniht*, from which the word knight comes, meant a household retainer: someone who followed a more important person. Records show that some knights were granted only very small amounts of land, similar to what a peasant family would have held from their lord. Some knights, though, were very powerful men, and nobles made sure their sons trained to be knights from an early age.

Historians think there were probably some 6,000 knights in Norman England. Their role was to guard their lord's property, ride out to combat any threat to their lord and, when required, to provide up to 40 days of **knight service** directly to the king. Rich and powerful knights (and their sons) would fight for their king as part of his royal court or as leaders of other bands of knights.

The knights were superior to other military units of the time. Cavalry charges became very effective against foot soldiers, once the Normans had developed the technology and training needed: couched lances in particular (see page 34). William needed knights as defence against the Vikings (we know Danish invaders feared to meet him in battle) and to fight wars in Wales and Scotland. He also needed them to fight other knights in wars with France.

Knights were important in suppressing opposition in England. Castles could operate both as places for knights to retreat to for defence and bases for launching attacks. The stables and smithies in castle baileys show that castles housed garrisons of knights, ready to ride out to suppress English unrest nearby.

Knights also had a social importance, replacing thegns as the under-tenants of their tenant-in-chief. Many knights would have been the local lord of the manor. Manors had manorial courts that tried minor cases involving tenants of the manor.

The nature of feudalism

Landholding

While Anglo-Saxon landholding had grown very complex over the centuries, William's imposition of what we call feudalism made things simple. The king owned all the land. William claimed this was just as it had been under Edward the Confessor, but this was not the case. In Anglo-Saxon England, many people had owned their land and were able to pass it on to their heirs. But, in Norman England, when a landholder died, the heir had to prove his or her loyalty to the king before they were allowed to reclaim it, as well as paying the king for the right to use the land. This payment was called a **relief**.

The relief system encouraged loyalty to the king. During William's rule, the king could decide how much the relief should be. That meant he could reward his most loyal followers by agreeing with them that their heirs would only have to pay quite small reliefs. Then, when the new heir took over tenure of the land, they had to pay the relief and also perform a ceremony of homage* to the king. The king could also threaten difficult or disobedient landholders with high reliefs, which might make it impossible for their sons to take over their estates when they died.

William was not bringing this system over from Normandy: it was a new situation for Normans, too. In Normandy, the barons had been used to their heirs inheriting their land as a matter of course. Since Normans were obsessed with building up their family's power and passing that power onto their sons, reliefs gave the king a lot of leverage. For William, reliefs were a key part of his strategy for reducing the power of potential challengers for the throne. However, reliefs quickly became a major source of discontent because the king could use them to make money as well as to reward loyal followers.

(see page 34)

Activities ?

1   Study the information on the role and importance of tenants-in-chief. Identify what the roles of the tenants-in-chief were (using the categories of social, political, economic and military).

2   For each role of the tenant-in-chief, explain why it was important in Norman England.

3   How big a change was the feudal system compared to how society was organised in Anglo-Saxon England? Identify at least three similarities and three differences.

Key term

Homage*

To demonstrate allegiance to another person publically.

Source A

Knights defend a castle from attack – an important part of knight service. From a 12th century bible.

Homage

When William granted land to a tenant-in-chief, an important ceremony of homage took place. The baron knelt before the king, put his hands between the king's hands and said: 'I become your man.' He then placed his hand on the Bible and promised to remain faithful for the rest of his life. The tenant-in-chief carried out similar ceremonies with his tenants.

Labour service

Labour service was about working the lord's lands in return for the use of land. The peasants would farm this land on top of their land service, for their own benefit.

There was a very wide range of labour service types that affected the majority of England's population.

Very frequently, these jobs involved helping with the ploughing of the lord's fields, sowing the lord's crops and harvesting them when they had grown. Other common forms of labour service were to provide a certain amount of produce each year; for example, planks and poles for fencing, honey from beehives or eels from rivers. People living in towns had to do labour service for any land that they worked outside the town.

Forfeiture

In the event that a land-user did not provide the service required of them, whether military or land service, they could forfeit their land (or have to pay a fine). Forfeiture was the punishment for breaking the relationship between the landholder and his or her tenant. It was designed to protect the lord's interests.

The Church in England

The Church's social roles and connection to government

The Church in Norman England had far-reaching social influences that went beyond praising God and helping others to do the same.

Figure 3.2 The Church's social roles.

The Church was also closely connected to Norman government.

- Because bishops and abbots were literate and well educated, they were often highly valued advisers to the king, both personally and in the royal council.
- Bishops often had the role of developing laws for the king and advising him on legal matters.
- Church clerks issued the king's writs and kept charge of the royal seal. Many bishops started their careers as clerks to the king: the king rewarded their service by these promotions.
- The most senior Church leaders, the archbishops, sometimes acted as the king's representative in negotiations. Archbishop Lanfranc acted as William's regent* while the king was in Normandy.

At first, William kept on many Anglo-Saxon Church leaders: he was crowned by the Ealdred, Archbishop of York, for example. He wanted them to support his message that he was the legitimate heir of Edward the Confessor, and was ruling England as Edward had done. But, after the rebellions of 1068–1070, William replaced almost all the Anglo-Saxon Church leaders with his own men. This extended all the way to the archbishops of the English Church. In 1070, Stigand, the Archbishop of Canterbury, was replaced by a reformer named Lanfranc.

Comparing the roles of Stigand and Lanfranc

There were many similarities in the roles of the last Anglo-Saxon Archbishop of Canterbury, Stigand, and his successor, Lanfranc.

Key term

Regent*
Someone appointed to act for a king or queen when they are underage, unable to rule because of illness or out of the country.

Extend your knowledge

Lanfranc and the pope
Lanfranc's reforms challenged the power of kings because the reformists said that the Church leaders in a country owed their ultimate allegiance to the pope, not the king. For William I, this was entirely unacceptable. Lanfranc made it clear that he served William rather than the pope. But it was a tension that continued to develop through the medieval period.

Lanfranc only
- Head of the Church in England
- Reorganisation and control of the Church
- Reinforcement of Norman rule
- Religious reform – separate politics from religion
- Church rebuilding

Roles Stigand and Lanfranc had in common
- Witan/royal council
- Legal expertise
- Ambassadors/ representatives of the king
- Defence of the realm
- King's secretariat and administration
- Tenants-in-chief – military and economic
- Shire courts and hundreds courts
- Administration of the Church
- King's household
- Advising the king

Figure 3.3 Roles of Stigand and Lanfranc in the Norman Church.

There were also key differences between Stigand's role as archbishop and Lanfranc's role that were connected to Lanfranc's reforms.

- Stigand had been a close ally of Earl Godwin, who had insisted on Stigand being made archbishop against Edward the Confessor's wishes. This appalled Church reformers like Lanfranc, who believed that the appointment of Church leaders should be made by those appointed by God.

- Stigand was Archbishop of Canterbury, but he had little control over the other archbishops or bishops outside his area. Different parts of the country did different things. For Lanfranc, this was unacceptable. He convinced William to make the Archbishop of Canterbury the head of the Church in England. That gave him the power to enforce discipline. Lanfranc revived Church councils and used them to push through his reforms.

- Stigand was also typical of Anglo-Saxon archbishops and bishops in that he was a '**pluralist**': he was bishop for two different areas: Canterbury and Winchester. The reason Stigand and the others did this was that each new bishopric (diocese) brought more land and more money. Stigand was also accused of **simony**: the practice of taking money in exchange for granting Church jobs to others. Lanfranc condemned these practices because he wanted the Church to stand above the corruption and money-grabbing of everyday life.

Lanfranc's reform of the Church

Lanfranc was an Italian monk, well known as a teacher and lawyer, who had run William's monastery of St. Stephens in Normandy. Lanfranc was heavily involved in religious reforms to separate the Church from entanglement with everyday aims of making money, gaining power and getting involved in sexual relationships. The reformers wanted those who worked for the Church to live a spiritual life of prayer and serving God. They also believed that the whole of society should be governed by the Church under a strict hierarchy: individual parish priests under the control of their bishops, bishops under the control of their archbishop, with one archbishop to be the leader of the Church in each country and that leading archbishop to be under the control of the pope in Rome.

- Lanfranc believed that Stigand and Anglo-Saxon Church leaders like him were not spiritual men at all. Anglo-Saxon parish priests lived as part of their community, getting married and having families. Lanfranc wanted his priests to be set apart from society, living spiritual lives. His councils passed laws banning marriage for the clergy and making celibacy (having no sexual relationships at all) compulsory for priests. (Lanfranc did relent and allow priests who were already married to remain so.)

- A Church council of 1076 passed Lanfranc's reform that court cases involving the clergy (priests and other ministers) should not be tried in the hundred courts (see Chapter 1, page 14), but should be heard in special Church-only bishops' courts. Trial by ordeal came under the Church's control, since it involved God's judgement. This was significant because it made the Church separate from all the rest of society and gave it a special role in the legal system.

- Anglo-Saxon cathedrals in isolated rural locations were knocked down and rebuilt in strategically important market towns (for example: Selsey to Chichester, Sherborne to Salisbury, Thetford to Norwich), so the bishop was installed in a more secure location with an overview over his area of control.

- Archdeacons became more and more common. Archdeacons were below bishops in the Church hierarchy, but above parish priests. Each archdeacon took a part of the bishop's diocese and enforced Church discipline within it. They had an important role in presiding over the Church courts. Archdeacons made it easier for the Church to get control over all the parish priests in a diocese.

- Lanfranc also introduced changes to Church ritual and brought with him from Normandy his personal collection of legal documents, which provided guidelines for understanding laws and developing new ones.

- Coming from a monastic background, Lanfranc oversaw a revival in monasteries in England, especially in the North. He promoted monastic values – dedication to a spiritual life, study and prayer, and the rooting out of corruption.

Normanisation and the Church

Within 50 years of 1066, every English church, cathedral and most abbeys had been demolished and rebuilt in Norman style.

This architectural change was accompanied by a purge of Anglo-Saxon Church leaders so that, after 1070, there was only one remaining Anglo-Saxon bishop – Wulfstan, bishop of Worcester. This did not mean that everyone who worked for the Church was a Norman – most parish priests were Anglo-Saxons – but the Church was quickly 'Normanised'. Above all, Normanisation meant that the Church was used to strengthen Norman control over England.

- Norman bishops and archdeacons influenced the messages people received about their king, their new lords and how God had favoured the Normans.
- The Church was a major landholder in England (one quarter of all land). Installing loyal Normans as bishops and archbishops secured these lands against possible Anglo-Saxon rebellions.
- Lanfranc's reforms extended the Normans' control over the countryside as parish priests came under stricter Church control and were made to follow Norman Church procedures and customs.

The 'Normanised' Church enhanced the king's power:

- New bishops did homage to the king. The king oversaw Church councils and his approval was needed for key decisions. Church leaders who failed their obligations could forfeit their lands.

- When a bishop died, the king appointed his successor. The king also received revenues from that Church land until the new bishop was appointed.
- William controlled communication between Church leaders and the pope in Rome. He would not permit any attempt by the pope to convince Norman Church leaders that they should obey the pope instead of him.

Exam-style question, Section B

'The main consequence of the Normanisation of England was that the king became more powerful'.

How far do you agree? Explain your answer.

You may use the following in your answer:

- the feudal system
- Archbishop Lanfranc.

You **must** also use information of your own. **16 marks**

Exam tip

Answers that do not go beyond the stimulus bullet points cannot access the highest marks.

The extent of change

Landholding was the basis of society and the economy. William's imposition of the feudal system looks like a huge change to the Anglo-Saxon way of life. But was it?

A summary of key social changes

Group	Anglo-Saxon England	Norman England
Slaves	About 10% of the population. Owned nothing; treated as property.	Normans thought slavery was wrong and sometimes freed slaves.
Peasants	About 80% of the population. Most peasants owed labour service to their lord, but some were 'free men' who could, if they wanted, take their labour to another lord.	Feudalism reduced the number of free peasants and tied everyone closer to complete dependency on their lord. Demands for more revenue from lords put more pressure on peasants.
Warriors	The thegns in Anglo-Saxon England: around 5–6,000. They owned five hides of land or more, as did the local lords. They owed military service in return for land.	The thegns were destroyed as a class and replaced by the vassals of the tenants-in-chief: often knights owing knight-service, who were often also lords of small manors.
Aristocrats	The great earls were serious challengers to the king in wealth and power, with thousands of thegns loyal to them and huge revenues from their extensive landholdings. They were the king's military leaders and swore loyalty to him.	Normans replaced Anglo-Saxons as earls, earldoms were made smaller and earls became tenants-in-chief like barons, bishops and abbots. All paid homage to the king in return for land and forfeited their lands if they failed the king.

THINKING HISTORICALLY **Cause and Consequence (3c&d)**

Causation and intention

1 Identify as many causes for the development of feudalism in Norman England as you can. Write each cause on a separate card or piece of paper.

2 Divide your cards into those which represent:

   a the actions or intentions of people

   b the beliefs held by people at the time

   c the contextual factors, e.g. political, social or economic events

   d states of affairs (long-term situations that have developed over time).

3 Focus on the intentions and actions of key people in the development of feudalism after the Norman Conquest: William I, William FitzOsbern, Bishop Odo and Lanfranc. For each person, use your knowledge to fill in a table, identifying:

   a their intentions in 1066

   b the actions they took to achieve these

   c the consequences of their actions (both intended and unintended)

   d the extent to which their intentions were achieved.

4 Discuss the following questions with a partner:

   a Did William deliberately design the feudal system, or did it emerge from other decisions he made?

   b How important are people's intentions in explaining the development of feudalism?

Continuity

Some parts of society and the economy showed more continuity than change. For example, in the villages, life would have continued much as it had before for most peasants. Their lives were dominated by the different demands of the agricultural year and surviving, if they could, the disasters of bad harvests and disease. The economic demands on many peasants may have increased, however. The Normans wanted to extract more revenue from England than had been the case under Edward the Confessor. This meant increased demands on all members of society.

Another example of continuity was the royal household. As well as the king's personal servants and bodyguard troops, the royal household included his administrative staff and personal advisers. Although William replaced the Anglo-Saxons carrying out these roles with his closest Noman followers, the roles themselves stayed much the same.

Most important of all to William must have been the geld tax. This was the key to extracting wealth from the whole of his kingdom. There was nothing like the geld

tax in Normandy. Previous Anglo-Saxon and Danish kings had set heavy geld taxes on their people. But William seems to have levied this tax more frequently and more heavily than ever before. William used this Anglo-Saxon tax to pull wealth out of England for the benefit of Normans and Normandy.

Change

One of the biggest changes for Anglo-Saxons must have been castle-building and the rebuilding of churches and cathedrals in stone. William promised that towns could keep all the trading rights and privileges granted to them by the Anglo-Saxon kings – they were very important to trade. But, at the same time, large areas of some towns and cities were cleared to make room for castles and for the construction of new churches and cathedrals. We know that Anglo-Saxon towns often burnt down in accidents, so townspeople were used to change. However, castles and cathedrals were very Norman and symbolised the power of the Normans.

Economically, Anglo-Saxon England had traded extensively, including with Scandinavian countries. The

Scandinavian trade was broken off under the Normans. This, and the Harrying of the North, must have had a serious impact on Danelaw areas, especially in Yorkshire. Parts of Yorkshire were still wasteland, from an economic point-of-view, nearly 20 years after the Harrying. However, while trade with Scandinavia decreased, trade with Normandy increased and big English cities (apart from York) seem to have grown rapidly under the Normans.

William was forced to remodel some social roles to remove the threats from the Anglo-Saxon nobility.

- Tenants-in-chief had many of the same roles as earls, but the king had much stronger control over tenants-in-chief in terms of the land they were allotted and the services they were obliged to provide. William did this to try and prevent men gathering enough power to challenge him as king – and here he faced threats from Normans as well as Anglo-Saxons.
- Thegns had been at the forefront of resistance to the Normans. Most of them were replaced by knights: Normans who depended on their tenants-in-chief for land and who owed knight service to the king. Although the thegns also owed allegiance to their Anglo-Saxon lord and made up the select fyrd, this was more than a change in personnel. The feudal system meant that most knights were much less independent than thegns. They were no longer often lords of a fortified hall with a church and lots of land. Their tenants-in-chief had much greater control over them if they did not fulfil their obligations. Most knights were quite poor and the service they did for the king involved guarding his castles, not heroic battles against Viking invaders.

Some historians have described the Norman Conquest as colonialism and Norman England as a military state. That may be extreme: both Anglo-Saxons and Normans seem to have adapted quite quickly and started to build a new Anglo-Norman culture together.

Because Anglo-Saxon England was much richer and more sophisticated than Normandy, the Normans rapidly adopted lots of English ways of doing things. But it is true that where change was greatest, it almost always related to gaining control over England's economy and reducing the chance of resistance to Norman control.

Summary

- Many of the aspects of feudalism were already present in Anglo-Saxon society, but William remodelled them to give him, as king, much greater control over society.
- Lanfranc's reforms of the Church were inspired by European reforms, but they worked to increase Norman control over England rather than allow the pope to challenge William's power.
- William was keen to use Anglo-Saxon roles and practices that helped Norman control over England. Sometimes this could be achieved by replacing Anglo-Saxons with Normans. Sometimes, bigger changes were required.

Checkpoint

Strengthen

S1 Identify three ways in which Lanfranc changed the Church in England.

S2 Describe two ways in which the feudal system of Norman England was different from how society had worked under Edward the Confessor.

Challenge

C1 Develop a comparison chart that identifies change and continuity between Anglo-Saxon England and Norman England under William I. Consider: the power of the king, landholding, the Church's influence, towns and villages, and the military.

C2 To what extent would you agree that there was more continuity than change in the Norman colonisation of Anglo-Saxon economy and society?

How confident do you feel about your answers to these questions? If you are not sure that you answered them well, try the activity on page 76.

3.2 Norman government

Changes to government

The government systems that had developed over the centuries of Anglo-Saxon England were often much more sophisticated than anything William had used in governing Normandy before 1066.

Having conquered a country with a much more advanced government, William chose to keep what worked. William then refined these systems so that they aided in controlling England, in increasing the power of the king and in extracting more revenue out of the English economy. For example:

- Norman government used the hide (and the wapentake) for working out tax obligations, like the Anglo-Saxons had done, and kept the shire and the hundred.

- William also seems to have maintained the Witan, or a royal council that worked in similar ways. When Norman England was facing Danish invasion in 1085, William gathered all the important landholders together in a huge meeting that appeared to be a large-scale Witan.

- The Norman economy used the Anglo-Saxon system of silver pennies and the royal treasury remained at Winchester, although William kept an even tighter control on who was allowed to mint coins.

Centralised power

William used the opportunity of conquest to centralise power in his hands. He owned all the land and was able to use grants of fiefs to reward followers and use forfeiture to punish anyone who acted against him.

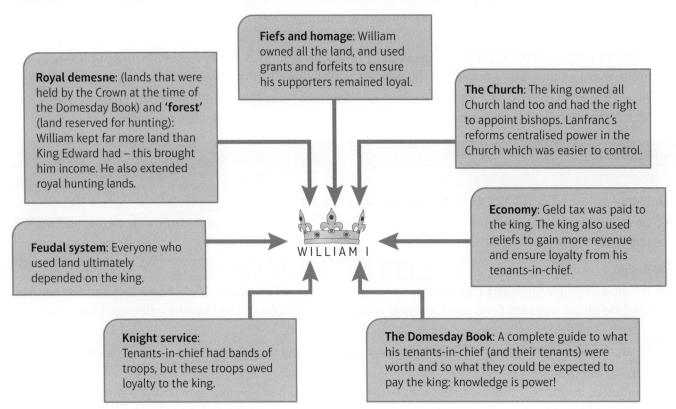

Royal demesne: (lands that were held by the Crown at the time of the Domesday Book) and **'forest'** (land reserved for hunting): William kept far more land than King Edward had – this brought him income. He also extended royal hunting lands.

Fiefs and homage: William owned all the land, and used grants and forfeits to ensure his supporters remained loyal.

The Church: The king owned all Church land too and had the right to appoint bishops. Lanfranc's reforms centralised power in the Church which was easier to control.

Feudal system: Everyone who used land ultimately depended on the king.

WILLIAM I

Economy: Geld tax was paid to the king. The king also used reliefs to gain more revenue and ensure loyalty from his tenants-in-chief.

Knight service: Tenants-in-chief had bands of troops, but these troops owed loyalty to the king.

The Domesday Book: A complete guide to what his tenants-in-chief (and their tenants) were worth and so what they could be expected to pay the king: knowledge is power!

Figure 3.4 The ways in which power was centralised in Norman England.

In Anglo-Saxon England, the power of the king was considerable, but there were other major landowners who had the wealth and influence to challenge the king: the earls. This had caused Edward the Confessor problems, for example:

- Edward had to depend on other earls' support when he wanted to exile Earl Godwin in 1051 and he could not then prevent the Godwins' return the next year.
- Earl Tostig's exile in 1065 happened because the earls agreed to it: Edward the Confessor had wanted them to lead an army against the Northumbrian rebels, but the earls had made excuses not to.

Reduced role of earls

William used this opportunity to reduce the power of the earls significantly and also the number of earls. Once his most loyal followers started being replaced, William made the earldoms smaller and more compact, or phased them out altogether (Wessex and Mercia, for example). Earls continued to have an important role in the military defence of strategically important borderlands. However, the special powers given to the Marcher earls immediately after the conquest were reduced. Earls were tenants-in-chief and subject to the same requirements as William's other barons. This reduction of power led to resentment from the heirs of some earldoms, as seen in the Revolt of the Earls in 1075.

The role of regents

Because William had two countries to run he relied on regents. William only used his most trusted followers as his regents. Lanfranc was William's regent during 1075 and used his powers to counter the Revolt of the Earls. During this time, Lanfranc was in regular contact with the king in Normandy, assuring him that everything was under control.

However, William tended to return as soon as he heard of trouble in England. Leaving a regent in Normandy (often William's wife, Matilda) was preferable to trusting a rebellious England to someone else, even someone as competent as Lanfranc. Perhaps this was because of the problems caused by his first two regents, Odo of Bayeux and William FitzOsbern. Their greedy and violent actions in 1067 (while William was celebrating his victories back in Normandy) contributed significantly to the waves of Anglo-Saxon resistance that followed.

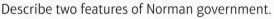

Exam-style question, Section B

Describe two features of Norman government.

(4 marks)

Exam tip

This question is about features. Make sure you identify two and add information about each of them.

The office of the sheriff and the demesne

In Edward the Confessor's reign, the shire reeve or sheriff had two main roles:

- He was the king's representative. The sheriff collected the revenue owed to the king from the shires and towns, including the geld tax when that was levied. The king's own estates, called his demesne*, were administered by sheriffs, too.
- He was the earl's representative, administering justice and ensuring the shire met its military obligations.

Key term

Demesne*

The land that the king or a tenant kept for his own use rather than granting it as a fief to an under-tenant. It is pronounced 'de-mean'.

After the Conquest, the sheriff's two main roles stayed very similar to how they had been before. But William changed the people doing the job: replacing Anglo-Saxons with Normans. Although William kept on some of Edward the Confessor's sheriffs at first (for example, Tofig of Somerset), they were almost all Normans by 1071. Some Anglo-Saxon sheriffs had joined the rebellions against Norman rule (for example, Maerleswein in Yorkshire), so replacing them with loyal followers would have been a priority for William.

Resentment against sheriffs

There were also some changes to the role of sheriff under the Normans:

Aspects of role	Anglo-Saxon sheriffs	Norman sheriffs
Importance	The king appointed the sheriffs, but the sheriff was less important than his earl. Sheriffs had to be careful not to upset their earl, even if there were problems to report to the king about the way the king's land was being treated.	The sheriff was still appointed by the king, but now the role had much **greater** power. Sheriffs answered to nobody but the king, so they were the undisputed leader of their shire. Norman sheriffs were very important men: some were tenants-in-chief; castellans were usually also sheriffs. The king required them to keep close control over their shires and those who failed him forfeited their role.
Law and order	Sheriffs were responsible for maintaining law and order in their shire. This worked by making each tithing responsible for the actions of its members: collective responsibility. Sheriffs presided over the shire court.	The Normans **kept** the same legal system, but added new laws to punish rebellion against Norman control, which the sheriff was also responsible for enforcing. Norman sheriffs lost some responsibilities when Church courts started to judge religious cases and when the feudal system led to manorial and baronial courts taking over legal issues relating to their administration.
Defence	The sheriff was responsible for the defence of his shire: for keeping roads and defences well-maintained and for gathering together the fyrd when the king needed it.	Sheriffs **kept** the role of organising the defence of the shire and gathering together the fyrd, but this system now ran alongside knight service, which the sheriff was not responsible for. The sheriff's main military role was usually as custodian of the king's castles in the shire.

- Sheriffs were entitled to a share of the revenues (due to the king) that they collected. They also kept some of the money paid in fines to the shire courts and possibly some of the geld tax that they collected for the king. This meant sheriffs could make a lot of money for themselves if they wanted to really squeeze the locals. (These sheriffs were not popular.)

- Sheriffs also paid a set sum to the king for the right to collect revenues from the king's estates. Sheriffs were able to keep any profits they made over and above that sum. This encouraged sheriffs to extract as much as possible from estates: also a recipe for being unpopular.

- Sheriffs were often at the forefront of the land-grabs following the Conquest, which must have been a focus for Anglo-Saxon resentment at Norman government. Because of their power, there was no one to complain to about their behaviour except the king.

The introduction and significance of the 'forest'

An important part of the sheriff's role in maintaining law and order in Norman England was in capturing and punishing those who broke forest law.

The introduction of the 'forest'

Early medieval kings loved hunting, and William was especially keen – the Anglo-Saxon Chronicle said that William loved the stags he hunted as much as if he were their father! In Anglo-Saxon England, the king was free to hunt wherever he wanted to across his own demesne, and this was the same for William's own lands in Normandy. However, the conquest of England gave William the opportunity to extend this hunting land.

Extend your knowledge

Complaints about sheriffs

Some sheriffs were particular figures of hatred: Sheriff Picot took so much land from the monks at Ely that the monastery described him as 'a hungry lion, a roving wolf, a crafty fox, a filthy pig, a shameless dog'. Henry of Huntingdon, who wrote a history of England in the 12th century, said 'the sheriffs and reeves, whose function it was to preserve justice and legality, were fiercer than thieves or robbers, and more savage to all than the most savage'.

Not only did William keep a lot more land as royal demesne than Edward the Confessor had (18% of the land was royal demesne in 1086), he also made new areas into 'forest', taking them away from other landholders. Forest land was not necessarily covered in trees, it meant land that was reserved for hunting and protected from other uses by law.

Because most of our records of the period were written by monks, we know the Church lost land to 'forest' in this way, but doubtless many other landholders were affected too. Whole regions were converted to 'forest', including the New Forest in southern England. Chroniclers at the time report large numbers of families being evicted from their homes as their land was reclassified as 'forest'.

Forest laws

Forest laws were introduced, protecting the animals that were best to hunt and also prohibiting damage to the vegetation that the animals needed. The king's favourite animals were deer and wild boar, though other animals were protected too. In order to make it easier to protect the animals from poachers, it was an offence to carry hunting weapons into the 'forest'. Hunting dogs were prohibited (and guard dogs had to have their front claws cut to stop them chasing animals) and there were many restrictions on cutting wood, clearing land and constructing buildings in the 'forest'. This made life difficult for people living within the forest, who depended on woodland for fuel and timber for construction, used dogs for herding animals (and as companions) and hunted rabbits and birds for food.

Activities ?

1   Identify two ways in which the role of sheriff under William changed from the role under Edward the Confessor.

2   Create a spider diagram of the ways in which the introduction of forest laws affected ordinary people living in forest areas. Were there any benefits (think of jobs that might be created)?

3   What does the word 'arbitrary' mean? To what extent was William's introduction of the 'forest' arbitrary and why was that significant for his role as king?

The significance of the 'forest'

The introduction of the 'forest' fits with other aspects of Norman control:

- It showed the power of the king to be above everything else. The term 'forest' came from the Latin for 'outside': these were areas 'outside' the usual way that society functioned.

- Extending the forest beyond his own demesne not only increased the amount of land the king controlled directly, it was also the equivalent of the land-grabs practised by William's sheriffs and barons. It made those actions appear more legitimate, as the king was the source of the law.

- Harsh punishments for breaking forest laws show the brutal side of Norman rule. Contemporary sources say those who unlawfully killed William's deer were to be blinded.

- As time went on, the forest areas became another source of income for the Crown, with all the fines paid by those accused of breaking forest laws and the sale of rights to hunt to others.

The unfairness of the royal forest, the way animals were given protection while people went hungry, built up over the years. The introduction of the 'forest' had consequences for the relationship between the king and the people, reinforcing the authority of the king.

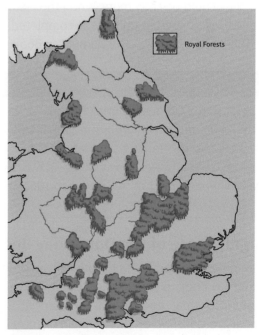

Figure 3.5 Map of royal forest lands as of c1200, when the forest was at its greatest extent.

The Domesday Book and its significance

At Christmas 1085, following discussions with his advisers, William ordered a survey of England. Men were sent to investigate the landholdings of each shire: who held what land, what taxes they owed the king and whether they could pay any more. When the results of this survey were written up (mostly completed by August 1086), the result was the Domesday Book.

Activity ?

Access translated Domesday Book records for your region (or a region you are interested in) at www.opendomesday.org. Working as a class, discover who the tenants-in-chief were, how much geld was owed and what changes you can find between 1066 and 1086.

The significance of the Domesday Book

There are different theories as to why William ordered the Domesday Book to be compiled, but it was certainly significant to Norman government for financial, legal and military reasons. No other European country had such a detailed survey of landholding for centuries. The Domesday Book provided a highly-detailed survey of almost the whole of Norman England.

Source A

The Anglo-Saxon Chronicle for 1085 describes the way the Domesday Book data was collected.

The king sent his men over all England into every shire and had them find out how many hundred hides there were in the shire, or what land and cattle the king himself had in the country, or what dues he ought to have in twelve months from the shire. Also he had a record made of how much [...] everybody had who was occupying land in England, in land or cattle, and how much money it was worth.

Extend your knowledge

The Domesday Book

There are around two million words in the Domesday Book, which was called 'Domesday' because its decisions were as firm as those of the Day of Judgement: 'Doomsday'. Some 1,000 tenants-in-chief are recorded (only 13 with Anglo-Saxon names) and around 8,000 under-tenants (only about 10% of whom were Anglo-Saxons).

Financial significance

Many of William's tenants-in-chief enjoyed special deals that meant they didn't have to pay geld tax on some of their land. It is possible that William had a plan to reverse some of these privileges as a way of extracting more money from his tenants. There were heavy geld taxes in 1084 and 1086.

Source B

The Domesday Book was compiled from detailed surveys made in (at least) seven regions. East Anglia was not included in the main book, so there are actually two Domesday Books, Great and Little Domesday. This is a picture of pages for Suffolk from Little Domesday.

The king received a lot of revenue from charging reliefs to new tenants or managing the estates of heirs who were too young to inherit. The way the Domesday Book is organised, with the holdings of each tenant-in-chief itemised by shire, makes it an excellent 'at a glance' guide for working out what the financial opportunities were whenever a tenant-in-chief died or forfeited their fief.

Legal significance

The Domesday Book includes many cases of Anglo-Saxons claiming that land of theirs had been taken from them. The Domesday surveys were made as fairly as possible, with all the key people in each hundred having a chance to say who really owned what. The Domesday Book therefore had a role in sorting out legal disputes over land, very important for William's claim to be just and fair.

Military significance

The council that William held about the Domesday Book was primarily called to discuss ways to counter a new Viking invasion threat in 1085. Although problems in Denmark meant the invasion never happened, William took the threat extremely seriously, bringing thousands of soldiers over from Normandy and housing them with landholders all over England. Although the Domesday Book does not record knight service, it may have been connected to this preparation, seeing how many extra soldiers each tenant-in-chief could provide.

Exam-style question, Section B

'The main significance of the Domesday Book was financial'.

How far do you agree? Explain your answer.

You may use the following in your answer:

- invasion threats
- the geld tax.

You **must** also use information of your own. **16 marks**

Exam tip

This question is about significance. Even if you think the Domesday Book **was** all about money, you still need to show **why** finance was more important than its other impacts.

Summary

- The Normans kept many Anglo-Saxon government structures and processes, but William centralised power so that no one responsible for English government had enough wealth or power to challenge his rule.
- The sheriff was the king's representative in the shire and also managed the king's demesne. William strengthened the sheriff's authority as part of the centralisation of power.
- The Domesday Book was a tool for William's central control. The summaries of detailed landholding surveys allowed William's government to see what feudal obligations were owed by his tenants-in-chief in almost every area of his kingdom.

Checkpoint

Strengthen

S1 Was William a fair or unfair king? Use an example to back up your answer.

S2 Describe two ways in which the role of the sheriff changed after the Norman Conquest.

Challenge

C1 Develop a comparison chart that identifies change and continuity between Anglo-Saxon England government and Norman government.

C2 Identify three ways in which William centralised government roles in England to increase his own power.

3.3 The Norman aristocracy

Culture

Norman aristocratic culture in England demonstrated wealth, power and superiority over the English. Normans did this primarily through buildings. While Anglo-Saxon aristocrats showed off with rich clothes and jewels, and lavished gifts on family members, the Norman elite put their money into jaw-dropping churches, cathedrals and castles. A 12th-century historian, William of Malmesbury, said that while the Anglo-Saxons lived like kings in miserable hovels, the Normans lived very simply and plainly in 'noble and splendid mansions'.

Within 50 years of 1066, every English cathedral, every church and most of the abbeys had been knocked down and rebuilt in the Norman style. The Norman aristocrats who paid for the building work were interested in making everything much bigger and more experimental than what had been before.

- Winchester Cathedral was the longest in Europe.
- Westminster Great Hall (rebuilt by William II) was the largest hall in Europe.
- William's White Tower (the Tower of London) was the biggest stone keep in Europe.
- Canterbury's priory had the largest stained-glass windows in Europe.

Extend your knowledge

Norman buildings
Some of the new Norman buildings fell down, for example, the bell tower at Old Sarum collapsed just a week after the new cathedral had been consecrated. The number of churches that collapsed is probably partly due to poor workmanship (there must have been a shortage of skilled masons with such a huge amount of rebuilding going on), but also because the Norman church builders were innovating and experimenting with church designs, but without understanding the strength of the foundations needed to hold their buildings up.

Aristocratic culture is often about showing off wealth: male Norman aristocrats shaved the backs of their heads, for example (in the same way that Anglo-Saxons had moustaches), because spending time on one's appearance was a luxury that common people couldn't afford. The same thing happened with the aristocrats' favourite leisure activity – hunting. The Normans introduced a complicated ceremonial way of butchering the animals they caught, to distinguish what they were doing from cutting an animal to bits in order to eat it.

The Normans also brought with them the culture of chivalry. Chivalry idolised the knight and created a

Source A

The interior of Durham Cathedral still has lots of Norman features. Building work began in 1093.

whole set of moral guidelines to accompany the bloody business of hacking your enemy to pieces. An example of chivalry in action is the way William treated captured enemies. While Anglo-Saxons would have killed them, William put them in prison – he was merciful.

Christian culture

Norman aristocrats were very religious, as well as being obsessed with warfare. Central to how this combination of Christianity and violence was possible was the idea of penance. All those who fought against the English at Hastings, for example, were ordered to atone for their sins: a year of penance for each man killed; 40 days' penance for each man wounded and, if they weren't sure how many English they had killed, they should build a church. By praying, doing penance and giving money to the Church, Norman aristocrats hoped to avoid eternal damnation in Hell for their sinful deeds in life.

Attitudes to the English

The Norman clergy threw out many of the old Anglo-Saxon saints' relics, not valuing them as sacred at all, and often destroyed the tombs of former abbots of monasteries, calling these revered holy men 'yokels and idiots'. This remark, and others recorded at the time, suggests that the Norman aristocracy considered themselves far superior to the conquered Anglo-Saxons. Chronicler Henry of Huntingdon said that, after the Conquest, 'It was an insult then even to be called English' and a 12th-century Norman is supposed to have called going to the toilet 'doing an English'.

Changes to landholding

Anglo-Saxon earls and thegns tended to pass on their estates to lots of different family members, but the Norman aristocrats brought with them a culture of a single heir inheriting the estate, keeping it all together. This attachment to land was reflected in Norman family names, which were often based on the places where the family had its estates.

Language

William tried to learn English, so he could understand land claims better, but had to give up given all the other claims on his time. When Lanfranc was appointed archbishop in 1070, he couldn't speak English.

In fact, written English rapidly all but disappeared: by the mid-12th century, it was completely replaced by Latin for legal documents (including writs) and Church documents, while the aristocracy talked to each other in French. English became a 'vernacular' language, spoken by the common people only, and was kept alive as a written language in just a few scattered centres like Peterborough, Worcester and Hereford.

Norman aristocrats probably never needed to concern themselves with learning English at all, using interpreters (called *latimers* in French), but everyone else (including their children, brought up by English nurses) could probably speak both languages. At the same time, many Norman aristocrats didn't understand Latin any better than English, so they wouldn't have understood the king's writs sent to them until they were translated by their clerks. Nor was this a reading culture: aristocrats listened to literature and memorised it rather than learning how to read for themselves. Fathers whipped their young sons when they witnessed land grants to help the sons remember the details.

Extend your knowledge

Hereward's French
Some Anglo-Saxon aristocracy spoke French: the legend of Hereward the Wake, for example, written in the 12th century, says that Hereward overheard the Norman plans because they assumed he was a peasant who didn't understand French.

Activities

1   Think about ways in which people show off status today, especially in music videos full of fast cars, jewellery, amazing houses and attractive party-goers. Storyboard what a Norman aristocrat would include in their bragging music video.

2   Write a diary entry for a Norman aristocrat observing life on the streets from their castle window. How would they have described the English people they saw below them?

3   Penance included fasting, abstinence from enjoyable activities and long periods at prayer. Why do you think Norman aristocrats, who were very proud of their 'best of the best' warrior status, also accepted that they should punish themselves for killing people?

Career and significance of Bishop Odo

Timeline

The career of Bishop Odo

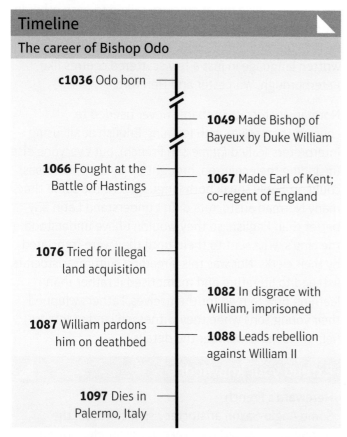

- **c1036** Odo born
- **1049** Made Bishop of Bayeux by Duke William
- **1066** Fought at the Battle of Hastings
- **1067** Made Earl of Kent; co-regent of England
- **1076** Tried for illegal land acquisition
- **1082** In disgrace with William, imprisoned
- **1087** William pardons him on deathbed
- **1088** Leads rebellion against William II
- **1097** Dies in Palermo, Italy

Source B

Bishop Odo as portrayed in the Bayeux Tapestry. It is thought that Odo commissioned the Tapestry.

Odo and the Conquest

Odo was William's half-brother: they had the same mother, Herleva. In 1049, William made Odo Bishop of Bayeux, even though his reputation was very poor. Odo was a major supporter of William's invasion, contributing 100 ships to the fleet, and fought at the Battle of Hastings.

William rewarded him with the earldom of Kent (forfeited by Leofwine Godwinson), and he also gained control of many other estates to become the second largest landholder in England, after the king. The Domesday Book records him holding land in 22 counties.

Significance

- William's most trusted supporters were his family members. They were rewarded richly.
- Odo's bad reputation (he was greedy and immoral) did not stop William from giving him important positions. William's first priority was loyalty.

Odo and power

Odo was co-regent during William's first absence in 1067. The Anglo-Saxon Chronicle says: 'Bishop Odo and Earl William [FitzOsbern] stayed behind and built castles far and wide throughout this country, and distressed the wretched folk, and always after that it grew much worse'. The Norman chronicler Orderic Vitalis says Odo had 'greater authority than all the earls and other magnates in the kingdom'. The Domesday Book shows him settling land disputes himself, and Orderic describes him as 'dreaded by Englishmen everywhere, and able to dispense justice like a second king'.

Significance

- Odo and Earl William [FitzOsbern] seem to have wrecked the king's attempts to gain Anglo-Saxon acceptance of his reign with their violent and oppressive actions.
- King William allowed Odo a lot of power; he was able to act as 'a second king'.

Odo in trouble

The Domesday Book records page after page of complaints against Odo for illegally seizing land, including Church land in Canterbury. In the end, it was Lanfranc who took the Church complaints against Odo to William, and a three-day inquiry in 1076 made Odo hand back their land.

In 1079, William sent Odo to Northumberland, following attacks from Scotland and the murder of the bishop of Durham. Odo laid waste to the region. According to chronicler Simon of Durham, Odo also pillaged cathedral treasures, and robbed and extorted everyone he could.

In 1082, Odo fell out of favour with William and was imprisoned. He was only released (in 1087) after William, on his deathbed, was convinced by Robert of Mortain (Odo's brother) to pardon Odo. William had freed other prisoners, like Morcar and Wulfnoth, the brother of Harold, without needing any such persuasion.

Historians are not sure how Odo got into such trouble. While it might have been his corrupt behaviour or an attempt at gaining the throne for himself, most historians think it was because Odo tried to take some of William's knights out of England with him for a journey to Rome (Odo saw an opportunity to get himself made pope). What actually happened is unclear, but taking knights from England went directly against William's centralisation of power. Knight service meant knights owed ultimate allegiance to the king. They were not the personal troops of their tenant-in-chief. No tenant-in-chief could be allowed to start putting together their own army, even if he was the half-brother of the king. If Odo thought differently, he had seriously misjudged the king.

Significance

- Odo went too far in his abuse of power (in the end), but probably only because he crossed Lanfranc: it isn't likely that many Anglo-Saxons who lost land to Odo ever got any back. However, it is significant that William was prepared to see the law enforced against a relative and a favourite.

- If Odo was imprisoned because of taking knights from William, that shows how seriously William took the idea that knights were loyal only to him, the king.

- The pope reprimanded William for imprisoning one of his bishops: Odo. William rejected the right of the pope to criticise what he did in his own kingdom.

In 1088, Odo led many barons in revolt against William II (see page 97). His willingness to act against his king suggests that his ambition for power had been the root of his troubled relations with William I.

Summary

- Anglo-Saxon aristocratic culture was replaced by Norman aristocratic culture.
- French took over as the language spoken by the aristocracy. Only common people spoke English.
- As a favourite of the king, Odo was untouchable. When he became a potential rival to William, all that changed.

Checkpoint

Strengthen

S1 Describe two features of Norman aristocratic culture.

S2 Why might the Revolt of the Earls in 1075 have influenced William to agree to an enquiry into Odo's activities?

Challenge

C1 What evidence would you use to support the argument that William protected Odo while he was useful to him, but then withdrew that protection once Odo became a threat?

How confident do you feel about your answers to these questions? If you are not sure that you answered them well, try the following study skills activity.

Activity

It is important to use facts and evidence correctly to support a clear argument, but another key skill is using your historical imagination: this can help you connect to the topics. Back up your theories with as much factual evidence as you can. Try to imagine yourself in Odo's position in 1082. What might he have thought about his situation?

3.4 William I and his sons

The character and personality of William I

A stern, brutal and greedy man

Source A

The Anglo-Saxon Chronicle for 1087 provides an obituary of William. It was written in Peterborough by a monk: we do not know much about who he was.

[William] was so stern and relentless a man that no one dared to [go] against his will. Earls who resisted his will he held in bondage. Bishops he deprived of their sees and abbots of the abbacies, while rebellious thegns he cast into prison. Finally his own brother he did not spare. His name was Odo. He was a powerful bishop in Normandy; he was the foremost man in England after the king. He had an earldom in England, and was master of the land when the king was in Normandy. William put him in prison.

William's toughness and determination must always have been part of his character. He was the illegitimate son of Duke Robert of Normandy, who made him his heir. When Duke Robert died in 1035, William was only around eight. He survived several assassination attempts by rivals as he grew up. Once he could lead his own armies, he was constantly at war, eliminating his rivals and strengthening his hold on Normandy. By 1066, he had a decade's experience of war, leadership, logistics* and military strategy, including cavalry tactics, castle-building and siege warfare. He had also built around him a brotherhood of loyal supporters.

Key term

Logistics*

The planning and organisation of supplies for troops and moving troops around.

As well as being stern and relentless, William was criticised for his avarice – his love of money and treasure, and his desire to own everything.

Source B

Norman chronicler William of Malmesbury, from his book *The Deeds of English Kings*, written c1125.

His anxiety for money is the only thing for which William can be blamed. He sought all opportunities of scraping it together, he cared not how. He would say and do almost anything, although it was unbecoming to his majesty, where the hope of money enticed him. I have no excuse to offer, except that through dread of his enemies he used to drain the country of money with which to deter or repel them. If strength failed, he could buy off his enemies with gold. This disgraceful calamity is still prevalent so that both towns and churches are forced to make contributions.

A religious king, a devoted husband

There were other sides to William, too.

- He was very religious. Although he was interested in what the Church could do for him, he also promoted Church reform with Lanfranc and founded abbeys.

- He recognised that his life had been brutal and is supposed to have repented on his deathbed:

Source C

Orderic Vitalis was a Norman monk writing c40 years after William's death, and was certainly not present at William's deathbed. He claims to record William's last words as being:

I've persecuted the natives of England beyond all reason, whether gentle or simple. I have cruelly oppressed them and unjustly disinherited them, killed countless thousands by famine or the sword and become the barbarous murderer of many thousands both young and old of that fine race of people.

- William took the English throne by force, but was always very concerned to be accepted as the legitimate heir of Edward the Confessor. He wanted to be a legitimate king.

- He was devoted to his wife, Matilda. When she died in 1083, he was said to have wept for days. He trusted Matilda: she served as regent in Normandy many times.

Relationship with his son, Robert

William and Matilda had many children, at least nine. The eldest was Robert, who was born around 1051. He was nicknamed Robert Curthose, 'short stockings' ('dumpy legs'), which is thought to be a mocking nickname given to him by his father. The relationship between William and Robert was difficult. Although Robert was a good warrior, William did not think he was ready to take control of Normandy, which was facing threats from its neighbours in the 1070s. Tensions flared between them.

- In 1077, following a prank in which his younger brothers, William and Henry, dumped water on his head, Robert started a real fight with his brothers that their father had to break up. Angry that his father did not punish the two younger brothers sufficiently, Robert and his men tried to take control of Rouen castle, then fled from William, who wanted them arrested.

- After William led troops against Robert and his men at Rémalard, Robert fled to Flanders. Then King Philip of France, William's enemy, installed Robert in a castle on Normandy's borders, from which Robert repeatedly launched raids, forcing William to raise an army against him.

- Matilda, unknown to William, had been sending money to her son behind William's back. When William found out, he was furious, although Matilda explained herself by saying that she would give her life for her children.

- At a battle in 1079, Robert and William fought against each other, and Robert knocked William off his horse and wounded him. With William defenceless on the ground, Robert gave his father his own horse and ordered him to retreat from the battle. This was a huge humiliation for William.

- Matilda organised a reconciliation between William and Robert at Easter, 1080. William restored Robert as his chosen heir for Normandy.

The events of Robert's revolt against William between 1077 and 1080 point to a key problem for medieval kings: princes who wanted power before their fathers were ready to let go of it.

Activities ?

1 Write your own obituary of William I. List his achievements and his problems, and invent quotes about him from those who knew him (or claimed that they did).

2 Pick one of the following questions about William and discuss how you would answer it. These are not questions that anyone knows the answer to for certain.

  a Did Edward the Confessor really promise William the crown?

  b Why did William commission the Domesday Book?

  c Was William truly religious, or was he only interested in what the Church could do for him?

3 In 1080, when Robert was back in his father's favour and named as heir to Normandy, the pope wrote to congratulate Robert and also offered him some advice about the duties of a son to obey their father. Write your own version of this letter, using your knowledge of William's character and the events of 1077–80 to help you.

Source D

The tomb of Robert Curthose, in Gloucester Cathedral.

William's death and the disputed succession

William's death and funeral

In July 1087, William led a raid into France, burning down the castle and town of Mantes. By this point in his life, William had grown very fat and, when his horse stumbled, he was thrown heavily against his saddle, causing internal injuries. He returned in great pain to Rouen. It was soon clear to his doctors that William could not survive his injuries. He suffered for many weeks before his death on 9 September. The moment he died, panic broke out. His barons rode away to secure their castles against attack, while the servants stole everything they could, including the furniture, leaving his corpse stripped of clothes on the floor.

At William's funeral, as the attendants attempted to squeeze William's body into its stone tomb, his bloated corpse burst open. The terrible smell drove everyone out of the cathedral. William's death was full of bad omens, suggesting to the people that God was still angry at his many sins.

The succession

Because of his drawn-out death, William had time to give his instructions about the succession to the throne of England and the dukedom of Normandy. William decided that Robert should succeed to the dukedom, despite all the trouble between them. In 1066, all the Norman barons had sworn their allegiance to Robert as William's heir. William put his trust in those oaths of allegiance.

William wanted his favourite son, William Rufus, to be king of England, but he was full of repentance at the violent way he had gained the crown. He said he would let God choose the next king of England.

William Rufus and the defeat of Robert and Odo

William Rufus left for England before his father's death. 'Rufus' means red in Latin; probably, William had red hair or red cheeks. He took with him a letter to Lanfranc from his father, recommending him as king. Lanfranc supported William's claim and he was crowned William II in September 1087 at Westminster. Lanfranc had such power in England, clearly, that no other council or Witan was required to authorise the succession.

Source E

William I as portrayed in the Bayeux Tapestry. Apart from the Tapestry, no portraits of William survive from his lifetime.

Odo and rebellion

William II faced serious opposition to his rule, however. Robert Curthose, as the eldest son, wanted to have England as well as Normandy. According to Norman custom, the eldest son inherited all his father's estates. There were good reasons why other important Normans would also have preferred one lord for both Normandy and England, instead of Robert as duke of Normandy and William as king of England. Barons often had lands in both countries and were worried about dealing with demands from two leaders, especially if William and Robert fought each other.

In 1087, Bishop Odo had been freed from prison. In 1088, he led a rebellion against William II, in support of Robert's claim to be king of England. Ambitious men like Odo thought Robert's weaknesses would be to their advantage: he would be a king they could more easily control. William was much more like his father and might well aim to reduce the barons' power.

Odo's brother, Robert of Mortain, joined Odo in revolt: the brothers controlled large areas of the south of England, including some heavily-fortified castles. Other rebellions broke out in 1088 alongside the main revolt:

- Small rebellions by Roger Bigod in Norwich and the sheriff of Leicester, Hugh de Grandmesnil; raids in Somerset and Wiltshire by Robert de Mowbray, Earl of Northumberland and in Gloucestershire by William of Eu.
- Medium-sized rebellions in the West, led by the Marcher earls Roger de Montgomery and Roger de Lacy, which were put down by a force assembled by Bishop Wulfstan (as in 1075).

Fascinatingly, however, the majority of Norman aristocrats, the bishops (except for William of Saint-Calais, bishop of Durham) and also the English population were against Odo's rebellion. Odo and Robert of Mortain took refuge in Pevensey Castle. William Rufus besieged the castle for six weeks, using local fyrd troops to attack the castle and prevent any supplies reaching the rebels inside. His tactics worked and he captured both his uncles, though Odo then escaped to Rochester castle.

Extend your knowledge

William Rufus and Robert Curthose

As William I had feared, Robert Curthose was not a strong leader. Without firm rule, the powerful, greedy barons of Normandy quickly grabbed power for themselves. William Rufus realised that they could be bought. He raised an English army but, instead of taking it to Normandy, he demanded from each knight the money they'd been given to live on during their service to the king and sent them home. William used this money to buy the allegiance of barons in eastern Normandy, forcing Robert to agree to rule Normandy together with his brother. This wily tactic turned the idea of knight service into something else: using feudal obligations to raise money for the king.

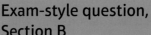

Exam-style question, Section B

Explain why William Rufus was able to defeat the rebellion of 1088.

You may use the following in your answer:

- Bishop Odo
- the Church in England.

You **must** also use information of your own. **12 marks**

Exam tip

This question is about causation. Quickly planning your answer before you start writing will help you develop your arguments clearly, making them easy for someone else to follow.

Odo held out there too, hoping Robert Curthose would come to support him. Help never arrived and he was eventually forced to surrender, as the castle ran out of food and was struck by disease. Odo was stripped of all his English lands and titles, and exiled.

William was wildly popular after the defeat of Odo and made many promises to his English subjects: lower taxation, an end to the 'forest' and the restoration of the laws of Edward the Confessor. This list of promised concessions is clearly what the English population had resented most about Norman rule. Unfortunately for the English, William went back on all of them.

Summary

- William I's character undoubtedly influenced the success of the Norman Conquest.
- However, William's strong personality created dangerous tensions between him and his eldest son, Robert. These tensions fed into a disputed succession and rebellion.
- Although many of the Norman aristocrats did not want different men controlling in England and Normandy, it is significant that most of them supported William Rufus against Robert.
- Even more significant is that the Anglo-Saxon population fought for a Norman king, too. William II's success was due mostly to the support of the fyrd, made up of Anglo-Saxons and 'Anglo-Normans'.

Checkpoint

Strengthen

S1 Suggest how William Rufus was able to get Odo to surrender, even though he was in a strong castle.

S2 Explain two reasons why William was doubtful that Robert would be a good duke of Normandy.

Challenge

C1 Review the Norman Conquest as a whole. List the changes brought about by the Conquest: social, political, economic, military and religious.

C2 Explain why you think the majority of Norman barons in England did not support Odo in his rebellion against William Rufus.

How confident do you feel about your answers to these questions? If you are not sure that you answered them well, try the following activity.

Activity

Remembering different individuals and their characteristics can be difficult. Create 'Top History' cards for Anglo-Saxon and Norman England, 1060–88. You will have to decide their scores for a set of key characteristics, for example: Military power, Political influence, Religious power; Economic strength. Key characters would include:

> Edward the Confessor, Harold Godwinson, Tostig Godwinson, Edgar Aethling, Harald Hardrada, William the Conqueror, a Norman knight, an English housecarl, a Norman footsoldier, an English fyrdsman, a Norman castellan, Archbishop Stigand, Earls Morcar and Edwin, Earl Waltheof, Hereward the Wake, Bishop Odo, William FitzOsbern, Roger de Breteuil, Ralf de Gael, Malcolm of Scotland, King Sweyn of Denmark, Archbishop Lanfranc, Bishop Wulfstan of Worcester, William Rufus, Robert Curthose and Matilda of Flanders.

Recap: Norman England, 1066–88

Recall quiz

1 'Land held by a vassal in return for service to a lord'. Which key term is that the definition for?

2 How many days a year was knight service for?

3 What was a relief?

4 Stigand was accused of pluralism and simony – which one of these was about appointing people to top Church jobs in exchange for money?

5 What was the demesne?

6 Describe two features of the role of a Norman sheriff.

7 In what year did William order the Domesday Book to be produced?

8 What language replaced English for written documents in Norman England?

9 Outline three key characteristics of William I's personality that help explain the success of the Norman Conquest.

10 What relation was Robert Curthose to Odo?

Activity   ?

> **CAUSATION**
> Change   *Consequence*
> *Continuity*
> Similarity   *Difference*
> Significance

These words are concepts used in asking historical questions. For example, causation is the concept behind questions asking you to explain why something happened. Other questions based on these concepts can be things like:

'To what extent did something change?' (change)

'To what extent did something stay the same?' (continuity)

'What was the consequence of something happening?' (consequence)

'How significant was it that something happened?' (significance)

'How similar was something to something else?' (similarity)

'How different was something to something else'? (difference)

Use each of the words in the word cloud to make a question about Norman England, 1066–88.

Exam-style question, Section B

'Of all the changes the Normans made in England, the most important was the change to the Church'.

How far do you agree? Explain your answer.

You may use the following in your answer:

- Lanfranc
- the feudal system.

You **must** also use information of your own. **16 marks**

Exam tip

This question is about importance. When you think about how important a change was, consider the difference that it made: its impact. The most important changes lead to the biggest amount of change.

Exam-style question, Section B

Explain why Bishop Odo lost power in 1082.

You may use the following in your answer:

- tenant-in-chief
- the Church.

You **must** also use information of your own. **12 marks**

Exam tip

This question is about causation. You can discuss the character and motives of William I as well as those of Odo to complete your answer.

Writing historically: writing cohesively

When you explain events and their consequences, you need to make your explanation as clear and succinct as possible.

Learning outcomes

By the end of this lesson, you will understand how to:

- use pronouns to refer back to ideas earlier in your writing
- use sentence structures to help you refer back to ideas earlier in your writing clearly and economically.

Definitions

Pronoun: a word that can stand in for, and refer back to, a noun, e.g. 'he', 'she', 'this', 'that', etc.

How can I refer back to earlier ideas as clearly as possible?

Look at the beginning below of a response to this exam-style question:

> It was changes in landholding that did the most to secure Norman control of England. How far do you agree? **(16 marks)**

> *Before William I introduced feualism, English land belonged to individual landowners, who could freely pass it on to their heirs. This was a major factor in securing Norman control.*

1. In the second sentence, the **pronoun** 'this' refers back to the first sentence. What could it refer back to?

   a. feudalism

   b. ownership of land

   c. passing land to heirs

   d. it's not clear – it could be referring to any or all of them.

One way in which you can improve the clarity of your writing is to avoid imprecise pronouns like 'this' and either:

- repeat the idea you are referring back to OR
- replace it with a word or phrase that summarises the idea.

2. Which of these would you choose to replace 'this' with to make these sentences as clear and precise as possible?

> *Feudalism   William's changes   William's changes to landholding   William's idea*
>
> *Before William I introduced feualism, English land belonged to individual landowners, who could freely pass it on to their heirs. This was a major factor in securing Norman control.*

3. Now look at some more sentences from the same response below. What could you replace 'This' with to make the sentences as clear as possible?

> *Feudalism was important in securing Norman control because the king owned all the land, he claimed relief before an heir could inherit, he could claim homage and knight and labour service, and force forfeitures. This enabled him to control his tenants directly.*

How can I structure my sentences to make referring back even clearer?

4. Look at three versions below of sentences written in response to the exam-style question on the previous page:

Version A

> *Before the introduction of feudalism, tenants could pass on their land freely to their heirs because they claimed a direct right to the land. This was a significant increase in control because people now only held the land on behalf of the king, who could take it away as easily.*

The pronoun 'this' is meant to refer back to this phrase – but, because it follows this clause, the writer seems to be suggesting that people claiming a direct right to their land significantly increased the king's control!

Version B

> *Tenants could pass on their land freely to their heirs because they claimed a direct right to the land before the introduction of feudalism. This was a significant increase in control because people now only held the land on behalf of the king, who could take it away as easily.*

Version C

> *Tenants could pass on their land freely to their heirs because they claimed a direct right to the land before the introduction of feudalism. This change in landholding was a significant increase in control because people now only held the land on behalf of the king, who could take it away as easily.*

Which version is most clearly expressed and therefore easiest to read? Write a sentence or two explaining your ideas, thinking about:

- the use of the pronoun 'this'
- the position of the idea it refers back to
- the use of a word or phrase that summarises the idea.

Did you notice?

When you read a text, you usually assume that the pronoun 'this' refers back to the piece of information that you have just read – not the one before that, or the one, two or three sentences ago.

5. Why are these sentences unclear and difficult to make sense of?

> *After Hastings William introduced feudalism. In Anglo-Saxon England earls and other landholders could resist the king as they held their land directly. This greatly increased Norman control.*

Improving an answer

6. Experiment with two or three different ways of rearranging and / or rewriting these sentence fragments to create sentences that explain as clearly as possible why Bishop Odo rebelled against William Rufus.

> *[1] There was a disputed succession [2] when William I died [3] because he divided his lands between his sons and the eldest (Curthose) wanted it all. [4] This resulted in Bishop Odo's rebellion.*

Preparing for your GCSE Paper 2 exam

Paper 2 overview

Your Paper 2 is in two sections that examine the Period Study and British Depth Study. They each count for 20% of your History assessment. The questions on Anglo-Saxon and Norman England are the British Depth Study and are in Section B of the exam paper. You should save just over half the time allowed for Paper 2 to write your answers to Section B. This will give you a few moments for checking your answers at the end.

History Paper 2	Period Study and British Depth Study			Time 1 hour 45 mins
Section A	Period Study	Answer 3 questions	32 marks	50 mins
Section B	Medieval Depth Options B1 or B2	Answer 3 questions	32 marks	55 mins

Medieval Depth Option B1 Anglo-Saxon and Norman England c1060–88

You will answer Question 4, which is in three parts:

(a) Describe two features of... (4 marks)

You are given a few lines to write about each feature. Allow five minutes to write your answer. It is only worth four marks, so keep the answer brief and do not try to add more information on extra lines.

(b) Explain why... (12 marks)

This question asks you to explain the reasons why something happened. Allow 20 minutes to write your answer. You are given two stimulus (information) points as prompts to help you. You do not have to use the prompts and you will not lose marks by leaving them out. Always remember to add in a new point of your own as well. Higher marks are gained by adding in a point extra to the prompts. You will be given at least two pages in the answer booklet for your answer. This does not mean you should try to fill all the space. The front page of the exam paper tells you 'there may be more space than you need'. Aim to give at least three explained reasons.

(c)(i) OR (ii) How far do you agree? (16 marks)

This question is worth half your marks for the whole of the Depth Study. Make sure you have kept 30 minutes to answer it. You have a choice of statements: (i) or (ii). Before you decide, be clear what the statement is about: what 'concept' it is about and what topic information you will need to respond to it. You will have prompts to help as for part (b).

The statement can be about the concepts of: cause, significance, consequence, change, continuity, similarity or difference. It is a good idea during revision to practise identifying the concept focus of statements. You could do this with everyday examples and test one another: *the bus was late because it broke down = statement about cause; the bus broke down as a result of poor maintenance = statement about consequence; the bus service has improved recently = statement about change.*

You must make a judgement on **how far you agree** and you should think about **both** sides of the argument. Plan your answer before you begin to write and put your answer points in two columns: For and Against. You should consider at least three points. Think about it as if you were putting weight on each side to decide what your judgement is going to be for the conclusion. That way your whole answer hangs together – it is coherent. Be clear about your reasons (your criteria) for your judgement – for example why one cause is more important than another. Did it perhaps set others in motion? You must **explain** your answer.

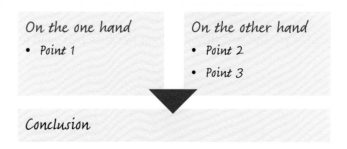

On the one hand
- *Point 1*

On the other hand
- *Point 2*
- *Point 3*

Conclusion

Paper 2, Question 4a

Describe **two** features of towns in Anglo-Saxon England. **(4 marks)**

Exam tip

Keep your answer brief. Two points with some extra information about each of them.

Average answer

Each shire had its main town called a burh which had strong walls. Towns were important for trade.

Identifies two features, but with no supporting information.

Verdict

This is an average answer because two valid features are given, but with no supporting information. Use the feedback to rewrite this answer, making as many improvements as you can.

Strong answer

The main Anglo-Saxons towns, called burhs were fortified with strong walls. These protected inhabitants from attack by Viking raiders.

Identifies a valid feature and provides supporting information (protection from attack) that is directly related to it.

Towns were important for trade, especially the burhs. In Anglo-Saxon England, all trade worth a certain amount of money had to take place in burhs by law, so that this trade could be taxed.

Again, the valid feature (that towns were important for trade) is supported with information that relates directly to why this was important.

Verdict

This is a strong answer because two valid features are given, with supporting information.

Paper 2, Question 4b

Explain why William won the Battle of Hastings.
You may use the following in your answer:

- knights
- tactics.

You **must** also use information of your own. **(12 marks)**

Exam tip

Focus on explaining 'why'. Aim to give at least three clear reasons.

Average answer

One reason why William won the Battle of Hastings was because his army included knights. Knights were warriors who fought on horseback. It took years of training to become a knight because special skills were needed to make a horse run at enemy troops and for the knight to use his lance as his horse charged. Norman knights charged into the Anglo-Saxon shield wall and chased after their troops.

Another reason was the Norman tactic of feigned retreat. This was when the Norman troops pretended to run away. This helped William to win because, when some of Harold's troops saw the Normans running away, they ran after them. The Anglo-Saxons were fooled by the tactic.

Another reason was William's leadership. When the battle was going against the Normans and it looked like they would be defeated, a rumour spread that William had been killed. He pushed back his helmet to show he was alive and shouted that they would all be killed if they ran away. This made his troops feel more confident and they fought back strongly.

William was very lucky to have won the Battle of Hastings in the end because it could easily have been him who was defeated, so probably luck is the most important reason after all.

This is an accurate description, but describing training and skills does not help explain why William won the battle.

Another valid point. However, it could be improved. It does not say what happened as a result, and so doesn't 'explain why'.

This is a relevant point and one not suggested in the stimulus bullets. This enables the answer to access higher marks. Providing an example gives support to the point being made. This is stronger than the first two paragraphs.

It is valid to say that luck was a factor in William defeating Harold, but the answer doesn't explain why William could easily have been defeated.

Verdict

This is an average answer because:

- information is accurate, showing some knowledge and understanding of the period, and adds a point additional to the stimulus (so it is not a weak answer)
- it does not analyse causes enough to be a strong answer
- there is some development of material, but the line of reasoning is not clear.

Use the feedback to rewrite this answer, making as many improvements as you can.

Paper 2, Question 4b

Explain why William won the Battle of Hastings. **(12 marks)**

Strong answer

Both armies in the Battle of Hastings were roughly the same size and both William and Harold were very experienced military leaders. It was William's leadership skills and use of sophisticated tactics that meant he ended up the winner.

While the Anglo-Saxons used a defensive shield wall, The Norman knights could move quickly across the battlefield. At the start of the battle, the hill up to the Saxon shield wall slowed their charge. But, when the shield wall weakened as sections of troops left the wall, the knights were able to cut through and run down fleeing enemies.

The key to William's victory was his ability to be flexible and try out different tactics. William was able to use his foot soldiers, archers and cavalry in different ways to attack the Saxons. For example, when direct cavalry charges failed, William used the tactic of the feigned retreat to weaken the shield wall. Harold's army included many general fyrdsmen, who were not highly trained or disciplined. When they ran after the 'fleeing' Normans, the Normans turned back on them, surrounded them and cut them to pieces. The loss of these troops weakened the shield wall.

It is clear that it was William's careful planning, knowledge of his troops and tactical know-how that ensured his victory. For example, warned by his scouts, he led his army out of Hastings early in the morning to prevent Harold taking him by surprise or bottling his troops up in the town. When his own troops were about to retreat after rumours of his death, William tipped back his helmet to show he was alive. This rallied his troops and shows how aware he was of what was happening across a chaotic battlefield. William's leadership skills won the Battle of Hastings.

An introductory sentence is not strictly necessary, but means it starts off with a clear focus on the question and the argument that is to come.

This starts off with a valid point, provides specific information in support and ends with an explanation of how it helped William win, linking it directly to the question.

This focuses on analysis rather than description, explaining why William's tactics were significant. Specific information is included, making a strongly-supported argument.

This adds a new point and supports it effectively, although there could have been a bit more emphasis here on 'explaining why'. Clear reasoning links it to the other factors, and a consistent line of argument is kept throughout.

Verdict

This is a strong answer because:

- the information is wide-ranging and precisely selected to support points that directly address the question
- the explanation is analytical and directed consistently at the question
- the line of reasoning is coherent and sustained.

Paper 2, Question 4c

It was changes in landholding that did the most to secure Norman control of England.

How far do you agree? Explain your answer.

You may use the following in your answer:

- tenants-in-chief
- forfeiture.

You must also use information of your own. **(16 marks)**

Exam tip

Consider points 'For' and 'Against' the statement and make a judgement. Be clear about your reasons for agreeing or disagreeing.

Average answer

When William became king he said that all the land belonged to him. This meant that everyone had to do what William said or they would have their land taken away from them (forfeiture). Because people needed the money from their land to live on, forfeiture was important in making sure everyone did what William said.

Another change to landholding was to do with knights. Lords had to provide knights for William in return for him letting them use 'his' land. That way, William had lots of knights to use in controlling the English population.

Another change to landholding was tenants-in-chief. Over half of the land in England was owned by 190 tenants-in-chief, and only two of them were Anglo-Saxons. William replaced the Anglo-Saxon landowners with Normans who were loyal to him. Anglo-Saxons who had no land or money couldn't lead rebellions.

So, overall, the statement is correct because the changes in landholding were so important in securing Norman control.

This uses the stimulus to make a valid point, linked to the question.

Another valid point, in addition to the stimulus points, that gives the answer a real boost. Again, it links back to the issue of control. However, 'how far do you agree' has not been answered, just relevant information given without analysis.

Good detail is added to this valid point, but a stronger answer would have weighed up other factors.

Although this has made valid points with strong knowledge, it does not analyse those points to address the question. There is no consideration of other factors.

Verdict

This is an average answer because:

- it shows some knowledge and understanding of the issue and it adds an additional point to the stimulus (so it is not a weak answer)
- it does not analyse factors enough or provide enough specific examples to support points
- it does not explain criteria for judgement clearly enough to be a strong answer.

Use the feedback to rewrite this answer, making as many improvements as you can.

Paper 2, Question 4c

It was changes in landholding that did the most to secure Norman control of England.
How far do you agree? Explain your answer. **(16 marks)**

Strong answer

Changes to landholding were central to how William secured his control of England. First and foremost, he changed who the key landholders were. Of his 190 tenants-in-chief, who owned half the land in England, only two were Anglo-Saxons: William oversaw a landholding revolution that took power and wealth away from Anglo-Saxons and into the hands of loyal Norman followers.

> This makes a valid point supported by specific information.

Forfeiture was an important part of how this control came to be imposed: anyone who rebelled against the king (even those who had fought against William at the Battle of Hastings) forfeited their land. The same was true for the under-tenants of the tenants-in-chief: if they acted against their tenants-in-chief, they could lose their land too. Norman control was passed down the feudal hierarchy in this way.

> This makes and supports a valid point with precise information showing good understanding of the period and the use of specialist terms: under-tenants, feudal hierarchy.

However, changes in landholding were also a cause of Anglo-Saxon rebellion against Norman control. Anglo-Saxons like Hereward the Wake rebelled against the Normans because of resentment at the loss of their land and because their old lords were replaced by Norman tenants-in-chief.

> Analyses 'how far' by considering weaknesses of the statement. Again, this is done by using a valid point and example. This makes the answer strong.

Nor were changes to landholding the only way in which Norman control was secured. For example, castles gave the Normans secure bases to dominate areas of England [answer gives some examples]. Without castles, it seems unlikely that Normans would have kept control over England.

> Uses additional information to provide another point that argues against landholding being the only important factor.

However, I believe that changes in landholding were the most important. Although resentment against the changes sparked Anglo-Saxon resentment, William responded to the rebellions by intensifying his landholding changes, replacing more Anglo-Saxon landholders with Normans through forfeiture. Castles were very important, but they were garrisoned by troops provided by the tenants-in-chief through knight service: the result of changes in landholding. Land was the key to wealth and power and William made sure that only those loyal to the Norman regime had it.

> A strong conclusion with a judgement that is backed up with solid analysis.

Verdict

This is a strong answer because:

- information is wide-ranging and precise
- factors are analysed and their importance is evaluated
- the line of reasoning is coherent and the judgement is appropriately justified with clear criteria.

Answers to Recall Quiz questions

Chapter 1

1 Edward the Confessor
2 Norway
3 Tostig, Gyrth, Leofwine [Wulfnoth and Sweyn also valid, but not mentioned in the chapter. Sweyn was Harold's eldest brother (Earl of Hereford), d.1052]
4 An Anglo-Saxon fortified town
5 A ceorl
6 Harold Godwinson, William of Normandy, Harald Hardrada and Edgar Aethling
7 Harald Hardrada (and Tostig)
8 King Harold II (Harold Godwinson)
9 One from the following: feigned retreat; cavalry (knights) charges against the shield wall; using archers, foot soldiers and cavalry flexibly; moving archers to closer range once the Anglo-Saxon shield wall had been broken up
10 Gyrth, Earl of East Anglia and Leofwine, Earl of the south-west Midlands (who was also Earl of Kent later)

Chapter 2

1 Edgar Aethling
2 Berkhamstead (and possibly also Barking for Earls Edwin and Morcar)
3 Hereford, Shrewsbury, Chester
4 Answers could include: the keep; the motte (earthen mound); wooden palisades; access to the keep (steps or bridge); the ditch; the gatehouse (or drawbridge)
5 Edgar (Maerleswein and Gospatric also escaped with him)
6 Burning crops in the fields, destroying seed crops and killing livestock to make life impossible in the region.
7 The three ways given in the text are: by forfeit, through the creation of new earldoms and other blocks of territory, and through illegal land grabs. Lands also got transferred through inheritance (Normans being made heirs to Anglo-Saxon lands) and through marriage (when Anglo-Saxon wives brought land to Norman husbands).
8 Ralph de Gael (Earl of East Anglia), Roger de Breteuil (Earl of Hereford) and Waltheof (Earl of Northumbria)
9 Ralph de Gael escaped to Brittany, Roger de Breteuil was put in prison for life by William, and Waltheof fled abroad. Waltheof was lured back, imprisoned, and then executed in 1076.
10 Archbishop Lanfranc – as William's regent

Chapter 3

1 A fief (or a feud)
2 40 days
3 A payment that a Norman heir had to make to the king when they inherited land.
4 Simony
5 The land that the king or a tenant kept for his own use rather than granting it as a fief to an under-tenant
6 Answers could include: the representative of the king; the leader of the shire; oversaw the shire court; enforced the law; responsible for organising the fyrd; responsible for the military defences of the shire
7 1085 (Christmas), the first drafts were ready in 1086.
8 Latin
9 Answers could include: he was relentless – he never gave up; he was brutal – he used excessive force, which helped crush resistance; he demanded loyalty – he imprisoned Odo once he appeared to challenge William; he had always had to fight for survival – which made him paranoid about any threat to his rule; he was religious – which helped gain the pope's support; he loved money – which drove him on to make the Conquest a success
10 Odo was Robert Curthose's uncle. Odo was Williams I's half-brother. Robert Curthose was William I's son.

Index

Acknowledgements

Picture Credits

The publisher would like to thank the following for their kind permission to reproduce their photographs:

(Key: b-bottom; c-centre; l-left; r-right; t-top)

Alamy Images: Glenn Harper 95, Justin Kase z12z 55, Pictorial Press Ltd 6, 11, QEDimages 90, Robert Harding Picture Library Ltd / Walter Rawlings 35, Skyscan Photolibrary 7t, The Art Archive 26, 58, World History Archive 25; **Bridgeman Art Library Ltd:** British Library, London, UK / British Library Board 8, 13, De Agostini Picture Library / M. Seemuller 96; **Corbis:** Alex Robinson / JAI 42; **DK Images:** Brian Delph 47, 49; **Getty Images:** Print Collector 17; **Mary Evans Picture Library:** Interfoto Agentur 22, The National Archives, London. England 74, 88; **The Master and Fellows of Corpus Christi College, Cambridge:** 77; **TopFoto:** British Library Board 63, World History Archive 7b, 92

Cover images: *Front:* **Alamy Images:** Robert Harding Picture Library Ltd

All other images © Pearson Education

Every effort has been made to trace the copyright holders and we apologise in advance for any unintentional omissions. We would be pleased to insert the appropriate acknowledgement in any subsequent edition of this publication.

Text

Extract in Source A on page 45 from *Anglo-Saxon Chronicle* 1972 ed., J. M. Dent (translated by G. N. Garmonsway) p.200, © 1972 Everyman's Library; Text extract on page 50 from *Anglo-Saxon Chronicle*, 1972 ed., J. M. Dent (translated by G. N. Garmonsway) p.200, © 1972 Everyman's Library; Figure 2.5 extract on page 51 from *Anglo-Saxon Chronicle*, 1972 ed., J. M. Dent (translated by G. N. Garmonsway) p.200, © 1972 Everyman's Library; Extract in Source A on page 68 from *Anglo-Saxon Chronicle*, 1972 ed., J. M. Dent (translated by G. N. Garmonsway) p.211, © 1972 Everyman's Library; Text extract on page 68 from *Anglo-Saxon Chronicle*, 1972 ed., J. M. Dent (translated by G. N. Garmonsway) p.211, © 1972 Everyman's Library; Extract in Source A on page 88 from *Anglo-Saxon Chronicle*, 1972 ed., J. M. Dent (translated by G. N. Garmonsway) p.216, © 1972 Everyman's Library; Text extracts on page 92 from *Anglo-Saxon Chronicle*, 1972 ed., J. M. Dent (translated by G. N. Garmonsway) p.200, © 1972 Everyman's Library; Extract in Source A on page 94 from *Anglo-Saxon Chronicle*, 1972 ed., J. M. Dent (translated by G. N. Garmonsway) p.219, © 1972 Everyman's Library.